When the Universe Cra[cks] framework for underst[...] and the church faced after COVID-19 was declared a pandemic. It's a timely and important book because it is honest, convicting, practical, and hopeful. When we are hit by life's disasters, it can be tempting to view our suffering as something to avoid or defeat. Instead, the book's authors encourage us to view disasters with Kingdom vision. Through the framework of the gospel, we can most fully process our pain, lament (alone and with others), serve those in need, and heal from trauma. As someone who studies disasters and has also lived through Hurricane Katrina and my own cancer diagnosis, I highly recommend this book.

JAMIE ATEN, PhD, founder and codirector of the Humanitarian Disaster Institute at Wheaton College

We are sorting out our lives amid unprecedented disruption, loss, and crisis—a true crack-in-the-universe moment. With much wisdom, global experience, passion for the goodness of God, and a love for Christ's Kingdom, the fine leaders in this compendium guide us through this perilous landscape. Use this book as a guide to the Kingdom conversations we must have to be moved forward into God's future.

DAVID FITCH, B. R. Lindner Chair of Evangelical Theology at Northern Seminary

To live in a fallen world is to live in a world full of crises. Although we live with that truth, it is still difficult to live into that reality. To help lean into the pain and discomfort of living in a cracked universe, Angie Ward assembled a diverse team to speak to the issue of living—not just surviving—as God's people in times of crisis. My hope is that God will use this project to help people understand, process, and faithfully proceed from whatever crisis they face now or may face in the future.

ED STETZER, executive director of Wheaton College Billy Graham Center

KINGDOM conversations

WHEN THE UNIVERSE CRACKS

LIVING AS GOD'S PEOPLE IN TIMES OF CRISIS

ANGIE WARD
GENERAL EDITOR

NavPress

A NavPress resource published in alliance
with Tyndale House Publishers

NavPress is the publishing ministry of The Navigators, an international Christian organization and leader in personal spiritual development. NavPress is committed to helping people grow spiritually and enjoy lives of meaning and hope through personal and group resources that are biblically rooted, culturally relevant, and highly practical.

For more information, visit NavPress.com.

When the Universe Cracks: Living as God's People in Times of Crisis

Copyright © 2021 by Angie Ward. All rights reserved.

A NavPress resource published in alliance with Tyndale House Publishers

NavPress and the NavPress logo are registered trademarks of NavPress, The Navigators, Colorado Springs, CO. *Tyndale* is a registered trademark of Tyndale House Ministries. Absence of ® in connection with marks of NavPress or other parties does not indicate an absence of registration of those marks.

The Team:
David Zimmerman, Acquisitions Editor; Elizabeth Schroll, Copy Editor; Olivia Eldredge, Operations Manager; Barry Smith, Designer

Cover photograph of geometric background copyright © Parameprizma/Freepik.com. All rights reserved.

Author photo taken by Denver Seminary, copyright © 2020. All rights reserved.

The author is represented by the literary agency of WordServe Literary, www.wordserveliterary.com.

Some of the anecdotal illustrations in this book are true to life and are included with the permission of the persons involved. All other illustrations are composites of real situations, and any resemblance to people living or dead is purely coincidental.

For information about special discounts for bulk purchases, please contact Tyndale House Publishers at csresponse@tyndale.com, or call 1-855-277-9400.

ISBN 978-1-64158-409-8

Printed in the United States of America

27 26 25 24 23 22 21
 7   6   5   4   3   2   1

CONTENTS

INTRODUCTION

As I write this from my home in Denver, Colorado, I can see a fine powder gently descending on my yard, dusting my grill and my patio furniture. I hold my mug of tea, take in the scene, and consider how I will adjust my plans and move my activities indoors for the next few days.

Sounds cozy, doesn't it? Except this powder isn't snow; it's ashes from the forest fires that are raging in the mountains just to the west of the city, ravaging our beautiful state. Smoke hovers in the air. My eyes itch. My throat is dry. It's hard to take a full breath.

What a fitting image as I write the introduction for a book about crisis. Between a pandemic, protests, politics, and natural disasters, it seems the whole world is on fire. I recently saw a meme titled "If 2020 Was a Scented Candle" that featured a photo of a porta potty in flames.

I realize that by the time you read this, the fires of 2020 may have died down. The world may have a widely available vaccine for COVID-19. Americans may have witnessed a peaceful transition of power in the Oval Office. Cities may have rebuilt the facades that were torn off by storms both social and meteorological. Firefighters may have contained the literal blazes that consumed millions of acres of land. But a quick review of history assures us that these crises will simply be replaced by new ones.

Into this ongoing unrest and uncertainty, I humbly offer you this book, the first in NavPress's new Kingdom Conversations series. As our world becomes increasingly turbulent, it is more important than ever to return to our root identity, orientation, and calling as followers of Christ. The Kingdom Conversations series dares to consider that any issue, no matter how complex, may be brought into conversation with what we know of God and of history and of one another, and in so doing, we can find new insight into how the people of God can persevere and bless through the great complexities of our time.

The contributors for this book were chosen with great care. We wanted a variety of voices—of ethnicity, gender, and vocation—but a shared heart: of love for God, for neighbor, and for God's people, the church. We looked for expert and experienced leaders whose writing would be fueled by missional passion yet warmed by wisdom. And we sought an integration of views, from global perspective to local practice.

I am absolutely delighted with the result.

Christine Jeske starts us off by defining crisis and explaining the nature and impact of crisis on individuals and societies. From there, D. A. Horton provides an overview of the COVID-19 pandemic, zooming his lens from the panoramic to the personal. Next, Efrem Smith pulls no punches as he reminds us that COVID-19 pales in comparison to the centuries-old crisis of racism, to which the church's silence has often been deadly.

Moving from the sociocultural to the historical, Marshall Shelley provides a review of the church's experience over millennia of crisis. (Hint: Crisis is nothing new.) Sean Gladding reflects on what we can learn from the example of our spiritual ancestors as described in the Scriptures. And Lee Eclov turns our attention to how Jesus prepared his people—including us—to face times of crisis.

Jo Anne Lyon then leads us toward a spirituality of crisis response, explaining how lament helps us love our neighbor. Kyuboem Lee continues the turn toward home by calling churches to radically reimagine and reshape themselves in light of postpandemic possibilities. Catherine McNiel invites us to get to work: to put on our boots, roll up our sleeves, walk out the door, and love our neighbors. And finally, Matt Mikalatos gently reminds us that what we're feeling is normal—crisis means hard times with no easy answers—and that God is here.

As you read this book, I hope and pray that your perspective will be enlarged, your faith strengthened, your spirit challenged, and your love expanded for both the God of the ages and your neighbor next door.

Angie Ward
GENERAL EDITOR

WHAT IS A CRISIS?

Christine Jeske

It was a crack in the universe to come home and see the destruction of Katrina. And it was in that moment that I said I was never leaving home again. You see that kind of destruction and your life will change, whether you want it or not.

COLETTE PICHON BATTLE

WHEN HURRICANE KATRINA HIT THE GULF COAST in 2005, Colette Pichon Battle was working as a lawyer in Washington, D. C. She rushed back to her home state of Louisiana. There she found that her Creole community was, as she put it later in a radio interview, "pretty much physically wiped out."[1] That crisis opened a "crack in the universe," sending her on a path to a new career. In the years that followed, she founded the Gulf Coast Center for Law and Policy where she advocates for equitable disaster recovery, climate justice, and economic development, especially among Native and Black communities.

A crisis is a crack-in-the-universe moment. As Pichon Battle said, it's a time when "life will change, whether you want it to or not."[2] In the book *People in Crisis*, psychologist Lee Ann Hoff and her colleagues describe what crisis is and isn't:

> Stress is not crisis; stress is tension, strain, or pressure. Predicament is not crisis either; predicament is a condition or situation that is unpleasant, dangerous, or embarrassing. Emergency is not crisis; emergency is an unforeseen combination of circumstances that calls for immediate action, often with life-or-death implications. Finally, crisis is not emotional or mental illness. *Crisis* may be defined as a serious occasion or turning point presenting both danger and opportunity.[3]

They go on to explain that in a crisis, we face circumstances that we cannot cope with using our "usual problem-solving devices." In a crisis, not only do we face factors beyond our control but we turn to our usual means of regaining control and discover it's not enough.

When we see crises as situations offering both danger and opportunity, we can understand both what makes a crisis so painfully difficult and how God works through crises. In this chapter, we'll look at three elements of a crisis: upheaval, revelation, and opportunity. We'll see that as terrifying as it is to reach the limits of our own control, upheaval is not all there is to crisis. Because a crisis brings us face-to-face with our own inadequacies—not just as individuals but as whole communities—a crisis is also the door to opportunity. As Christians, our calling is not just to survive a crisis, it's to ask God how to fully turn to him amid the dangers, the revelation, and the opportunities of a crisis.

Crisis Brings Upheaval

A crisis disrupts aspects of life we usually take entirely for granted. The effects of a crisis run deep. Like an earthquake, a crisis rattles both the visible portions of a building and the deep recesses beneath the surface. That unseen shaking can crack building foundations, burst water and gas lines, and trigger volcanic or tsunami events beneath land or sea. Likewise a crisis affects not only our everyday, visible, and conscious decisions but also the subterranean aspects of our being: our norms of social interaction, our sense of identity, the narratives we use to make sense of life, and our foundational spiritual beliefs.

Throughout our lives, we are guided by sets of norms and rituals that we follow without having to ask deep, probing questions. Social life is held together and given order by these expected behaviors and the meanings we attach to them. For example, in the culture I grew up in, I learned without thinking that a handshake is a way to communicate welcome of a new acquaintance. I learned that going out for coffee with someone is a way to develop casual, honest conversation and friendship. I learned expectations about where to sit when I arrive at work, how a classroom will be organized, and what to do on the way in and out of church.

In everyday life, our cultural norms are like the pavement, painted lines, and road signs that make up our transportation routes. As we drive, we don't have to decide who drives on which side of the road or who stops at an intersection—the painted lines, stop signs, and stoplights tell us who does what, and if we follow those rules, we expect to be safe and get along. Sure, we face decisions in everyday life, but usually those decisions are like choosing which way to turn at an intersection. We don't typically have to decide whether to drive through a corn field or a river.

When these norms, habits, and rituals are taken away, we feel the tension in ways we do not even know how to name or express. A crisis is like trying to drive through a city where pavement and road signs are washed away, stoplights no longer function, and no one knows for certain how to get from point A to point B. In some crises, like Hurricane Katrina, this is quite literally the situation people face—physical infrastructure is destroyed. But in any crisis, we face a similar situation in a metaphorical sense. The roads of our social norms and rituals wash away, and the dilemmas we face are not just a matter of mapping an alternate route on a GPS app. As COVID-19 spread across the world, suddenly rituals like shaking hands, going out for coffee, and sitting together in meetings and classrooms disappeared overnight. We had to relearn—as a community—what it means to move through life.

Not only do our shared habits and rituals help us get stuff done but they also give meaning to our lives and help us understand who we are. We take for granted that others around us roughly agree on these behaviors. Knowing that our behaviors are predictable and accepted cements both our relationship to others and our sense of who we are. If you ask me who I am, I might tell you that I am married and care for my two kids. I work as a college professor and participate in church activities. I go out for coffee and gather for book clubs with certain friends on a regular basis. These things are not just what I do; they tell me and others who I am. The combination of all those shared expectations, norms, and behaviors makes up our culture. Most of these rules were created without people ever stopping to plan out what the rules would be. They come about so gradually that we are not conscious of them having a beginning, an end, or any alternative. We all benefit from having these rules—most of the time, anyway. In a moment, we'll come back to the problem of what happens when those unspoken rules don't benefit people, but suffice it to say, those rules make us who we are as individuals and as a society.

A crisis, at its core, is a moment when the old rules don't work, shaking our understanding of what to do and who we are. One of the earliest sociologists, Émile Durkheim, called this state of "normlessness" *anomie*.[4] In his lifetime during the late nineteenth century, Durkheim watched a massive social shift as industrialization transformed European and American ways of life. Within a generation, normal life went from shared agriculturally based work in small communities to industrial employment and consumption choices beyond what previous generations had imagined. It wasn't a crisis that hit overnight like a stock-market crash, but it brought about a slowly unfolding crisis as old ways of life disappeared.

Durkheim noticed that while much attention was focused on economic changes, much deeper changes were also happening. Industrialization didn't just change people's jobs: It brought about the loss of a whole system of morality. Government exercised less control over everyday life, occupational guilds dissolved, and religion played a lesser role in public life. As the old systems of regulating morality crumbled, Durkheim described what he called a "liberation of desires" causing a "state of crisis and anomie."[5] To track these changes, Durkheim looked at the statistical rise in suicides and divorces that corresponded to industrialization. He realized that mental and emotional health were not just results of our individual circumstances—they could rise and fall in tides with the shifts of our entire society. In the short run, at least, Durkheim found that anomie would be painful. Much of his research focused on this question: Will society be able to survive these changes?

In much of the Western world today, people learn to think of themselves primarily as unique individuals, making choices that dictate the consequences of their own lives. In a crisis, though, people realize that they are not in control. Social circumstances affect us, whether we like it or not. I remember listening to a friend who lives in Philadelphia describe a scene that played out in her neighborhood in the summer of 2020. So many of the city's sanitation workers were calling in sick or quarantining from coronavirus that trash pickup fell days behind. Garbage on streets overflowed from trash bins, stinking and humming with flies and maggots. Rain filled garbage bins, making them impossibly heavy, and as few as 25 percent of sanitation workers were left on duty. On one hot summer day, a sanitation worker, in my friend's words, "a big burly dude," sat down on the side of the street by a pile of rancid rubbish and began to weep. Neighbors came out to talk with him, and eventually a manager came to relieve him for the day as he still shook with sobs. Crisis is when the basic systems we rely on—from trash pickup to sending kids to school—have collapsed, and no individual is immune from the emotional weight of carrying on.

Much of what scares us about crises is the upheaval. When norms, habits, and our very sense of identity are disturbed, we experience emotional, physical, and economic burdens. As much as some of us like variety in our lives, nobody wants the kind of brokenness that comes with crisis. But another part of what scares us is the next aspect of crisis: the revealing. As old systems are thrown into upheaval, the foundational ideas that produced these systems are laid bare. In the case of Philadelphia's trash pickup crisis, people witnessed the crumbling of a system they had taken for granted,[6] and it unearthed deeper questions: *How can a community work together to solve problems we can't fix as individuals? What should government do? What does a job have to do with a person's ultimate purpose? What's the fairest way to distribute scarce resources?*

Ultimately a crisis reveals new facets of some of our

deepest age-old questions: *Am I my brother's keeper?* (Genesis 4:9) and *What good is it for someone to gain the whole world, yet forfeit their soul?* (Mark 8:36).

Crisis Is Revealing

In March of 2020, as my email inbox was overflowing with notifications about canceled events and in-person gatherings moving online, I plugged in my earbuds and went for a run. Scrolling through the many podcasts that were now focused solely on COVID-19, I chose one from the *The Bible Project*, appropriately titled, "Apocalypse Please," with the descriptive line, "Is this the apocalypse?" I was intrigued. These early days of facing the pandemic surely felt like what people tend to call apocalypse—the coming of the end of the world. But as hosts Tim Mackie and Jon Collins explained, "apocalypse . . . does not mean end of the world." The English word *apocalypse* is transliterated from a Greek word meaning "revelation." The word is used across the Bible, not just about God revealing the new heavens and earth but for various times when God suddenly gives the ability to see reality in ways that people previously could not see it.[7]

Crisis brings about upheaval, but in that upheaval, we also receive apocalypses. In their podcast, Mackie and Collins highlighted a few revelations happening in America during the early days of the pandemic. Families and couples who now had to spend every moment together discovered harmful patterns in the ways they had been relating to each other. People out of work recognized how they had idolized career success.

Patterns emerging in infection and death rates revealed racial and ethnic disparities in health care and resource access that had existed for generations.

During the coronavirus crisis, God revealed to people realities about both individual lives and culture. Often those cultural patterns were painful to see because of the very fact that people now faced the reality that social factors mattered—humans are not and never have been totally free individuals. Other times they were painful because they revealed how we as individuals had been complicit in accepting cultural norms and systems that harmed ourselves and others.

One revelation America faced at a cultural level was that even the best science has limits. As predictions of when we would bounce back from the pandemic stretched further and further into the future, Americans realized that there could be no guarantee that scientists could cure our bodies, either now or ever. In hospitals, health-care workers faced the reality that even if they could access enough ventilators and other technologies, many people would die from COVID-19. The coronavirus revealed the lie beneath the common Western expectation that life would keep getting better.

As human beings, we make sense of events by fitting them into narratives. We assume that certain events follow one after another, and causes and effects are predictable along certain lines. In the West, one of those narratives often used to make sense of events has been called the *redemptive-self narrative*.[8] As Christians, we tend to think of believing in redemption as all good, but in this narrative, it's not Jesus who leads the redemption—it's ourselves. Since the Enlightenment, systems of education and science in the West have been geared toward breaking down problems, testing hypotheses, and working hard to find answers. That way of solving problems has indeed cured innumerable diseases and brought modern technologies that enhance people's quality of life. But the dominant culture also teaches people to credit human ingenuity for overcoming any problem and to expect that over time, society will keep making itself stronger, richer, smarter, and better.

This narrative differs significantly from the biblical flow of history. Throughout the Old and New Testaments, groups of people rise and fall in power through cycles involving human sin and God's overarching command of history. Crises often reveal people's dependency on the redemptive-self narrative. In a crisis, not only does the present look bleak, but we have to be honest about the fact that the future might not get any better. In these moments of revealing, we can see the world through a different narrative: *What if history and progress are in God's hands, not humans?*

During the moments of financial crisis, another narrative that is often revealed is that for many people, especially those in the middle class, work holds the central place in our identity. To be out of work or seemingly failing at work—whether in a situation like a coronavirus quarantine or long term—touches deep nerves not only because of economic insecurity but because a dominant Western way of thinking equates work with human value. Among middle-class people, introductions often begin with people telling what they do for work. The narratives that saturate Western society teach people that when able-bodied adults are not working, there must be something morally wrong with them. This has never been true—at any time in history, plenty of people are out of work for no fault of their own or for noble purposes. And yet for many Americans, it takes a crisis to reveal this.

Crises also often reveal our fears and the ways we assign blame. In cultural anthropology classes I taught in the spring of 2020, we began studying patterns of social-media posts to notice patterns of responses to COVID-19. Several students began tracking how people talked about masks. They noticed that masks became first a revealer of xenophobia, and then a political symbol. In the early days of the pandemic, White Americans were subconsciously racializing masks, imagining them as something only Asians wore. For many Americans, masks triggered thoughts that blame for the disease could be assigned to "foreigners," not ourselves. The pandemic unearthed long-standing prejudices of Asian Americans and Asians as perpetual foreigners, dangerous outsiders, and competitors. As one student wrote in an article she later published on the topic, "Asian Americans are framed as 'dangerous virus carriers,' magnifying their existing alienation."[9] She quoted the anthropologist Mary Douglas: "Fear of danger tends to strengthen the lines of division in a community . . . the response to a major crisis digs more deeply *the cleavages that have been there all the time*."[10]

A few months later, masks had become another symbol of

cleavage, this time of political polarization. From conservative to liberal parts of the country, the patterns of who wore masks revealed not just the choices of individuals but the patterns of who we trusted, who we identified with, and how strained were relationships even within one nation.

Ultimately the revelations that happen in a crisis lay bare our spiritual state. We are forced to face uncomfortable realities. Our social systems are broken. We do not control our own lives completely, and when we do, we mess up. We are sinners, desperately dependent on the triune God. How we respond to these realities further reveals our relationship with God. Do we tighten our grasp on fears and sins? Or do we step into the light and become what God calls us into in this moment?

Crisis Offers Opportunity

When people talk about crisis, much of what usually comes up is along the lines of what Émile Durkheim saw amid anomie—suicides, divorces, and social breakdown. But Durkheim also believed that anomie was a pathway into new kinds of social order, and he was fairly optimistic that new social orders could be as good as or even better than old ones. Christians see similar patterns throughout history and Scripture: A crisis is a time for remaking our communities and ourselves, and if we invite God into that process, we need not fear.

Over half a century after Durkheim's research, an anthropologist named Victor Turner picked up on Durkheim's question of what happens when a society goes through turmoil.

Turner noticed something about crises: A social crisis isn't all that different from other kinds of transition that people go through all the time. The kind of normlessness and social upheaval that happens in a hurricane is somewhat like the kind of upheaval that an individual goes through when, say, they graduate from college or get married. In all those situations, people have to leave behind an old way of life and enter a new one. Between one way of living and another, we pass through an in-between time that Turner called *liminality*. The word originally described a threshold, the space in a doorway that is neither in nor out. Liminal times can be scary and downright dangerous because we hover between systems. We leave behind old norms and roles and haven't yet entered new ones.

But societies figure out ways to carry people through liminality. As Turner studied rituals around the world, he noticed that what happened in unsettled times wasn't all bad—in fact, a lot of what happened there was beautiful, inspiring, and powerful. Liminality kicks us out of old routines, which not only gives us those apocalyptic epiphany moments but also sets us up to do something about what's revealed to us.

In ordinary life, people resist changing old systems because change can require us to face old traumas or release structures that benefitted us to the detriment of someone else. Systems and norms are hard to change—no one individual can do it alone, and even social movements that are desperately needed just aren't that easy to get going. So, too, as individuals, we cling to our old habits. And so we often go on following old ruts long after their usefulness fades away, even when they hurt people.

But in liminality, our inertia against change is already broken. Recall that most of the time, norms and rituals help us function in society, but not always. Plenty of systems go wrong, like the health-care systems that leave millions of Americans without reliable access to affordable health care, or racial divisions across neighborhoods, schools, and churches. In times of crisis, not only are those systems revealed but often our normal modes of behavior are so unsettled that we have to rebuild new systems. In the rebuilding, we just might make things better. The shake-up of liminality is like spring cleaning for social systems.

In this way, crisis brings not just the dangerous confusion Durkheim saw in anomie; it can bring a necessary, renewing force in society. In the early months of the pandemic, my own family realized that in scrapping all our usual extracurricular commitments, we had the energy to start new healthy and fun habits like daily walks, Wednesday crossword puzzling, and Fancy Friday dress-up days. When these types of habit changes multiply on a societal scale, a lot can change.

One opportunity that often comes in crisis is that our shared problems override the usual hierarchies and barriers that divide us, and we reach out to each other as equals in previously unheard-of ways. It's the phenomenon we experience in my native state of Wisconsin when blizzards hit. Suddenly neighbors who never spoke are out clearing each other's driveways and delivering warm meals to those without power. A crisis can be a portal to human connections and a reminder of our shared unity as human equals. Turner and his wife, Edith, both anthropologists who converted to Catholicism as adults, call this sense of equality and unity *communitas*, and they wrote that ultimately, it can offer a glimpse of the Kingdom of God.[11] They wrote that liminality often brings "experiences of unprecedented potency," "sacredness," and "collective joy."[12] In other words, when this anthropologist couple compared all the ways humans deal with transitions and crises, they saw there Christ and his Kingdom.

Looking back at the way the world coped with COVID-19, we see many times when crisis sparked communitas. Celebrity John Krasinski's show called *Some Good News* became an overnight viral hit on YouTube. Viewers watched what felt like a home video of him sitting in front of his daughter's hand-drawn "SGN" logo, hearing stories of people across the world caring for one another amid the pandemic. Not only did the show give viewers the sense that Krasinski and the other stars who called into his show were all just "one of us" but it also reminded viewers that goodness was possible in a crisis. Viewers around the world loved watching stories of everyday acts of kindness not just because they showed us what we wanted to happen but also because in many communities, this extraordinary caring *was* happening.

The early weeks of the pandemic created space for communitas. People started GoFundMe efforts to support artists, restaurant workers, hair stylists, and other out-of-work service providers. We saw messages of hope and gratitude spring up everywhere, from sidewalk chalk to murals, balcony music ensembles to free online concerts. When George Floyd's tragic death by police brutality reminded the nation once again that systemic racism still threatened the well-being and survival of people of color, historic numbers of demonstrators turned out on streets and engaged in some part of the long, hard work of undoing the racism that permeates society. In the very act of socially distancing, people were rediscovering and embracing the reality that we are all in this together and we cannot do this alone.

Opportunity is not the same, though, as prediction. Opportunity means there are options that some will take and others will not. There is no guarantee that crisis brings out the best in people—it can also bring out our worst. In many instances, the pandemic widened inequalities in wealth, education, and health-care access and worsened domestic violence and mental-health situations. In a society-wide crisis, systems will undoubtedly change, but whether for good or for evil is yet to be determined. In the chapters that follow, we will read more about how to respond to times of upheaval with a willingness to open our eyes and actively invite God's Kingdom to come in the middle of today's opportunities.

One paradox of responding to a crisis is that a crisis calls for both hard work and relinquishing control. Unless people commit to the long, slow work of rebuilding systems in ways that reflect the Kingdom of God, any euphoric sense of unity that might happen in a crisis will quickly fade as we return to old, selfish habits. But at the same time, a crisis reveals that we do not have complete control over our choices and outcomes. The words of James 4:13-14 (BSB) never ring so true as when we come to a crisis:

> Come now, you who say, "Today or tomorrow we will go to this or that city, spend a year there, carry on business, and make a profit." You do not even know what will happen tomorrow! What is your life? You are a mist that appears for a little while and then vanishes.

In crisis, we have the opportunity to adjust our inflated sense of agency—that is, our expectations of what we are capable of.

In research I conducted over several years in South Africa, I interviewed dozens of people about the ways they sought better lives amid some of the world's highest unemployment rates and most entrenched racism.[13] One common trend I noticed among people who said they were experiencing a good life even amid difficult circumstances was that they acknowledged that a good life was not entirely in their own control. Social scientists call this temporary release of control over a situation *abeyance of agency*.[14] This doesn't mean giving up and doing nothing. In fact, the people who talked about the role of God helping them through tough situations often were the most active in working for good. In admitting that the outcome was not fully in their control, they had the freedom to try without being terrified of failure. Instead of grasping as much control over their own lives as possible, people who thrive through a crisis practice some forms of abeyance agency. They learn new ways to trust both in other people and in a higher power. In a pattern that repeats again and again throughout Scripture, as people desperately cry out to God and commit to following him, God guides them to new and good paths.

For the Joy Set Before Us

In the years after Hurricane Katrina as Colette Pichon Battle became an advocate for disaster relief and prevention, she realized she would have to learn how to persevere in that tough work without resorting to fear or hatred. She recalls looking at the ways people of her Louisiana Creole, Black, and Native ethnic heritage have persevered through generations of struggle. She realized, "We are not a people who are energized by hatred. I come from people who were energized by joy."[15]

The same is true of all Christians. We are a people who are energized by joy. We tend to associate crisis with pain, not with joy. But at the center of what was perhaps the biggest crisis of all time—the crisis of God atoning for the sin of humankind—we find Christ, dying on a cross, not out of fear or hatred but "for the joy set before him" (Hebrews 12:2). What is crisis? It is upheaval, a moment of revealing, and ultimately, if we meet God there, it is opportunity to be motivated by the joy set before us.

2

NOTES ON A
RECENT CRISIS

D. A. Horton

How quickly the world can change.

In December 2019, the American public was notified that the earliest case of what would become known as COVID-19 was traced to China.

By January 13, 2020, the World Health Organization confirmed the first case outside of China in Thailand.[1]

By July 2020, the United States led the world in both confirmed COVID-19 cases and deaths.[2]

By mid-December 2020, it was reported that 188 countries had over 72 million cases, with over 1.6 million deaths, and in the United States alone, COVID-19 became the leading cause of death.[3]

In my lifetime, I had never seen anything stop the world in

its tracks for an indefinite period of time. From global economies to individual households, COVID-19 fundamentally altered nearly every aspect of life as we knew it. In an attempt to capture what took place, I have structured this chapter around four different views of how COVID-19 disrupted society and how churches, parachurches, and individual Christians responded. The first view is *panoramic*, as it frames a global picture. Second is the *peripheral*, sharing nuances of three ethnically marginalized populations in America. The third is *pastoral*, with insights from our local church. Lastly is a *personal* view as I open the doors of our home and candidly share our life rhythms in response to changing circumstances.

The Panoramic View

On February 11, 2020, the World Health Organization announced the name COVID-19 as the respiratory virus that had already been contracted by 42,708 people in China, 1,107 of whom had died.[4] One month later, on March 11, due to the rapid spread and severity of COVID-19, the World Health Organization characterized it as a global pandemic.

Two days later, on March 13, 2020, President Trump declared a national emergency regarding COVID-19.[5] The day before President Trump declared the national emergency, there were 1,645 people from forty-seven of the fifty United States infected with COVID-19 and globally more than 125,000 cases with over 4,500 deaths and at least 68,000 recoveries.[6] Celebrities began to share their infected status via social-media outlets, Ireland suspended school for a few weeks, and professional sports in America were canceled. With no vaccine available, the world was told to embrace precautionary measures that altered billions of lives around the globe to slow the spreading of a disease.

Social distancing became a household term as fear gripped the world. Global travel restrictions not only impacted the workforce of that industry but also readjusted the world's supply and demand of goods. Primary (e.g., agriculture, oil), secondary (i.e., manufacturing), and tertiary (e.g., education, finance, health care, etc.) sectors were all disrupted, leaving companies and national governments scrambling to find ways to pay employees who were not allowed to show up for work.[7] Fears of a global recession set in as the darkness of the unknown hovered over humanity at large.

Many around the world turned to their faith in creative ways that had been taboo to some and unheard-of by others just weeks before the pandemic hit. Israeli Jewish leaders found innovative ways to perform balcony *minyans*, as well as online Passover observance.[8] Learning from the MERS-CoV outbreak, the government of Saudi Arabia banned prayers in mosques and mandated that prayers be done at home for the first time in the kingdom's history.[9]

In Poland, Christians of Orthodox, Protestant, and Roman Catholic traditions all suspended services in person and moved toward in-home or online practicing of the faith but remained committed to serving the sick and elderly.[10] In Uganda, COVID-19 produced a rise in prophecy with mixed claims, some saying the pandemic would not touch born-again

Christians in the country, while other pastors claimed God said they would heal those who get it—to which social critics challenged the pastors to go to hospitals and heal those infected.[11] Around the world, amid constant change, people sought to engage expressions of faith to find ways to cope.

The Peripheral View

Marginalized ethnic communities are often hit especially hard during times of social disruption. COVID-19 shows no prejudice in who it infects, and as fear gripped some, they lashed out at people different from them. Often, when resources are needed to engage a specialized ministry focus, parachurch organizations come alongside churches to help meet needs. COVID-19 had an unforeseen impact on parachurches, however: Their financial support took a nose dive, thus presenting roadblocks for them to be able to assist churches. The peripheral view in this section will bring attention to different marginalized communities and how the church responded in love to help meet their needs, as well as how parachurch organizations pivoted to meet the needs of their targeted populations.

Asian Americans and Pacific Islanders

In the United States, hate crimes targeting Asian Americans, who were blamed for bringing COVID-19 into the United States, rose at alarming rates. The A3PCON (Asian Pacific Policy and Planning Council) reported on April 24, 2020, that since launching the "STOP AAPI HATE" reporting center, they had received almost 1,500 reports of coronavirus discrimination from Asian Americans.[12] By the month of June, more than 2,120 hate crimes had been reported.[13] Videos of people antagonizing Asian Americans in public spaces went viral, and it was not helpful for President Trump to repeatedly refer to COVID-19 as the "kung flu" and "Chinese virus."[14]

Amid the hatred rose a plea from Asian American Christians for ceasing this treatment. Pastor Raymond Chang, alongside Michelle Reyes, Jeff Liou, Russell Jeung, Jay Catanus, Jessica Chang, and seven other Asian American pastors, scholars, and thought leaders drafted and released the Statement on Anti-Asian Racism in the Time of COVID-19.[15] This statement plowed a path for the creation of the Asian American Christian Collaborative (AACC), which "seeks to encourage, equip, and empower Asian American Christians and friends of [their] communit[ies] to follow Christ holistically."[16] The AACC has produced video series, articles, and other resources from a distinctly Asian American Christian perspective to bless the church and society.

African Americans

By April 2020, more than 50 percent of COVID-19 cases and nearly 70 percent of COVID-19 deaths in Chicago took place in the African American community.[17] In Michigan, "African Americans [were] 3.8 times more likely to die of COVID-19" than people of other ethnic descent.[18] In earlier phases of COVID-19 research, obesity and body mass index were not considered; however, later on, the CDC (Centers for Disease Control) said individuals with a body mass index (BMI) of greater than 40 were classified as "high risk," and studies have shown that obesity is a significant factor in COVID-19 severity among African Americans.[19]

Dr. A. R. Barnard said that COVID-19 caused the Black Church, which is steeped in beautiful tradition, to realize they were caught "off guard" by stay-at-home orders and realized their lack of a "digital footprint."[20] Gleaning from their deep-rooted history in employing innovation for meeting together to provide hope, many Black Churches such as Greater St. Stephen United Church of God in Brooklyn turned to Zoom, YouTube, and Facebook to stream services for the first time. Generational differences also gained more distinction because, as social scientist of religion Cleve V. Tinsley IV noted, "those who have been through Jim Crow may go to church no matter what,"[21] so finding alternative methods during stay-at-home orders provided opportunity for both innovation and generational unity. Early in the onset of shelter-in-place orders, Dr. Willard Maxwell Jr., pastor of the New Beech Grove Baptist Church in Newport News, Virginia, held services by preaching at a podium in the church's parking lot, streaming it live on Facebook while also allowing members to sit in their parked cars, at a safe distance from each other.[22]

Latina/os

Assessing COVID-19's impact on Latina/os is complex due to variations in data based on where those infected lived. In general, Latina/os "have among the highest age-adjusted rates of COVID-19-associated hospitalizations" and "account for approximately one in five of all confirmed COVID-19-related deaths in the U.S. with known ethnicity/race data."[23] Compared to other ethnicities, the United States Latina/o population is considerably younger and overrepresented in specific workforce areas, specifically in manufacturing facilities. This reality caused many Latina/os to be classified as "essential workers"[24] during the early onset of COVID-19, which allowed them to become extremely vulnerable. Many Latina/os exposed to COVID-19 worked *essential* jobs that did not offer adequate health care, and those who spoke only Spanish admitted to being afraid of seeking medical attention due to their immigration status.[25]

In response, churches began to open up and partner with physicians to help serve the Latina/o population, even allowing their buildings to serve as space for providing mental-health services.[26] Churches also helped meet the essential needs of the Latina/o community by providing food. Cecelia Bernal, food bank director for the food ministry at Church of the Redeemer in the Baldwin Park neighborhood of Los Angeles, who before COVID-19 would open the food bank once a month, moved to opening eight times a month and also added home deliveries for seniors and those who can't drive to the church to get food.[27]

Parachurch Organizations

Similar to churches, parachurch and Christian nonprofit organizations experienced a decline in financial support due to COVID-19. It was reported that 20 percent of Christian nonprofits faced a hiring freeze, 14 percent reduced staff to part-time hours, and as time went on, optimism regarding financial support through the crisis waned greatly.[28] All religious nonprofits now had to wrestle through their participation in the CARES Act for funding relief since many do not have large amounts of capital.[29]

Yet, in spite of the financial need, Christian parachurch organizations and nonprofits knew the mission to serve those in need remained, even if the money was not coming in. To help meet the felt needs of those suffering through COVID-19, parachurch organizations stayed focused on creating and distributing resources through creative measures.

- Crown Financial Ministries developed resources specifically to equip people with financial insights and budgeting skills for those laid off during COVID-19.[30]

- On May 2, 2020, Cru Inner City provided food, masks, snacks, and water to thirty-three partnering churches throughout Los Angeles County to distribute to those in need in their immediate neighborhoods.[31]

- COVID-19 forced the Youth for Christ Houston chapter to stop in-person ministry opportunities to incarcerated youth. Jonathan Frost, the executive director of Youth for Christ Houston, partnered with a local Chick-fil-A to take lunch to the staff and kids at the Galveston County Juvenile Justice Center, in addition to partnering with Honore's Cajun Café to cater lunch for the 330 staff members at the Harris County Juvenile Justice Center.[32]

- The North American Mission Board (NAMB) of the Southern Baptist Convention not only provided electronic and financial resources to struggling churches, but they also regularly highlighted how churches in Canada and the United States were adjusting their missional responses to COVID-19.[33]

The Pastoral View

COVID-19 provided local churches, denominations, and networks with a prime opportunity to recapture the roots of the Christian faith, when Jesus followers met in large rooms inside of homes instead of designated church buildings.[34] The Anglican Alliance created a webpage filled with resources Anglican Christians could access while church buildings were closed. The Anglican Alliance shared timely counsel by reminding Jesus followers: "The church does not close, only the building. Because we are the church, the living body of our Lord Jesus, and we are everywhere."[35]

Striving to help churches remain faithful in their local communities, Wheaton College published a manual to help churches think through rapid changes regarding restrictions and the uncertainty of what was to come. Nuances that were considered in this manual included: creating an internal health-care team, how to communicate to vulnerable groups, how to partner with other local churches, and adapting to changing needs.[36]

The Episcopal Relief and Development podcast interviewed several ministry leaders around the country to hear how they partnered across denominational lines with churches in their communities to minister to the homeless in their cities during COVID-19. Members of churches made masks to give away, and churches pooled resources to purchase food and water to give freely to the homeless in their cities. The expression of unity among churches was common in each of the cities, and the desire for these partnerships to continue after churches are allowed to reopen was expressed, as well.[37]

As it relates to our local church's response, March 8, 2020, was the final time we were able to gather as a local body indoors. My close friend Carlos Gaxiola, an elder in training, preached through Acts 4:1-31, and my responsibilities for the day were minimal. After March 8, the *next gathering* never took place. In response, our leaders provided our members with a number of resources:

- Home Bible-study content that families and those living with roommates could work through together during shelter-in-place orders.

- Links to corporate online prayer gatherings with other local churches who were part of the Long Beach Church Collective.[38]

- Updates on our church website to make members and visitors aware of COVID-19 information, as well as forms to report price gouging and lists of places where people could find food to help feed their families.

- Home worship services for the duration of Holy Week.

Lastly, the elders informed our members that the focus moving forward would home in on *finances* (providing assistance to those in need), *awareness* (making known the needs of those inside our community who are outside of our church), *innovation* (finding creative ways to minister to our city), *togetherness* (promoting small, approved online and in-person gatherings throughout the week), and *healing* (from emotional, mental, and racial trauma experienced during COVID-19). The framing of our focus was captured in the acronym FAITH.[39]

The Personal View

My wife, Elicia, and I knew that we were facing an opportunity for the discipleship rhythm in our home to literally become a twenty-four seven operation. This meant an end to the up to three-hour-per-day interruption of family time for my commute from Long Beach to Riverside, where I serve as an assistant professor at California Baptist University (CBU). All three of our children would no longer spend eight-hour days at school. We were in this together for an indefinite period of time.

At first, we treated the shelter-in-place order like that liberating week between Christmas and New Year's. About a week of this behavior fueled a desire to have more structure during the work week. Elicia broke out the old homeschool materials and began giving instruction to all three of our kids, ages sixteen, twelve, and seven. I recorded lectures online for my students while handling church-related work most days, as well. Elicia also developed "the three Cs" for our weekends. The first C varied—on Saturdays, we each had *chores*, and on Sunday, we all had *church*. Once the first C was completed, we were to find something *creative* to do that didn't involve electronics, and then we could *chillax* (a hybrid of *chill* and *relax*). We even created a "March Madness" bracket of nearby restaurants we would order from, rate them, and see the winner move on to the next round. (Of course, my #1 pick, In-N-Out Burger, was victorious.)

COVID-19 prevented me from traveling to preach and teach at different events, which dried up a necessary income stream for our family. We took a massive hit financially and asked God to provide us with wisdom on how to make ends meet. Within a few weeks, Elicia was offered a job at The Grove Community Church in Riverside, only fifteen minutes from CBU. Elicia and I shared the news with our children, and we wept tears of mixed emotions, knowing a transition was on the horizon.

Shepherding our children through the transition from Long Beach to Riverside brought us closer as a family. In the Lord's providence, our closeness helped us grieve with hope when my mother-in-law, Norma Cisneros, lost her battle to COVID-19 on December 8, 2020. That morning, Elicia called me on FaceTime so I could read Psalm 116 to Norma. I told her I loved her and to run the streets of gold into the arms of her Savior, Jesus. Elicia said she was going to let me go so she could play worship music for her mother and sister Elaina, who was also in the hospital room. Within two minutes of my last conversation with Norma, she was in the presence of the Lord. Her transition to glory was accompanied by MercyMe's "I Can Only Imagine."

One lesson we learned during COVID-19 was how to be *realistically thankful*. If we truly believe every good and perfectly timed gift is given by God (James 1:17), we must steward what he gives while fighting to remain thankful (Colossians 3:15-17; 1 Thessalonians 5:18). God the Holy Spirit (Romans 8:1-3) supplies every believer with the strength to remain thankful while living in a realistically broken world. Perhaps being *realistically thankful* is God's desired response from his global church, who not only endured COVID-19 but may encounter unforeseen socially disrupting, life-altering events in the future.

◆　◆　◆

It's evident that our world was not ready for the changes to everyday life that COVID-19 brought. Yet, in spite of this, God's people around the world chose to lean in to the tension of living on Jesus' mission in light of a global pandemic.

Churches from denominations that refused to work together before now found themselves partnering to meet the needs of their immediate neighbors. Parachurch organizations and Christian nonprofits still mobilized to meet the needs of the marginalized.

While it is true that some churches were forced to close and have not yet reopened, it is also true that small churches that might have closed found a spark that led to a desire to hit the restart button. At the same time, while COVID-19 seemingly drove people into deeper commitments to their faith than ever before, a by-product of this newfound zeal was public disagreements on how to respond to local government restrictions on indoor gatherings.

The future of the church in America has yet to be written. COVID-19 has forced the Lord's bride to change pens and find innovative ways to tell the gospel story. Although what was once normal is now something of the past, one reality Christians should agree on is the words of Isaiah reminding Jesus' followers, "The grass withers, the flower fades, but the word of our God will stand forever" (Isaiah 40:8, ESV). No matter what surprising reality hits the world and the church, Jesus will remain faithful in building his church, and neither the gates of hell nor the nuances of a global pandemic will ever prevail.

3

CRISIS WHILE THE WORLD MARCHES ON

Efrem Smith

IN 2020, THE CORONAVIRUS PANDEMIC (COVID-19) changed everything, and at the same time, it exposed what hasn't changed.

It seems that no crisis—whether natural disaster, terrorism, or virus—can pause the myriad of challenges that seem to hold us captive in this upside-down and broken world. Systemic racism, political polarization, and violence as a primary conflict-solving strategy continued to plague our world in ways that no virus could stop. COVID-19 wasn't a strong enough global crisis to cause, even for a short period of time, racial reconciliation or a broader national unity. It didn't lead deeply divided political parties to commit to nonpartisan and civil dialogue, rally leaders of nations all over the world to find collaborative solutions, or place a brief moratorium on violence.

This chapter will focus mainly on the ongoing social crisis of systemic racism and its impact specifically on African Americans. It alludes to the intersections of politics and the continued racialized divisions within the body of Christ. It also explores the responses to the deaths of unarmed African Americans broadly, and the divergent responses of the African American and evangelical church in particular. Finally, this chapter presents the Black Church as a missional gift to evangelicalism in presenting a long-standing, settled, humble, and apostolic-prophetic theology. This is an ecclesiology settled on obedience to a sovereign God, humble in the face of an unsettled world, and also committed to bringing the righteousness and justice of the Kingdom of God to bear on whatever crisis comes its way.

I realize that it is not only Black bodies who are deeply impacted by the racialized realities of the United States of America. Brown bodies are impacted by unresolved and nonexistent bipartisan immigration policies that contribute to children being ripped from their parents and caged at the borders. Asian American bodies are impacted by the racial profiling and physical attacks caused by referring to COVID-19 as the "kung flu" by the US president and members of his administration. I acknowledge these realities and, at the same time, focus in this chapter on Black bodies and the Black Church because I write as a Black Christian pastor and a product of the Black Church. I am aware of other forms of racial oppression, but I purposely focus on the experience that I know personally. I also believe that the Black Church and the Black Christian experience can serve as a blessing to the entire body of Christ. Historically and presently, it is already a given that the White church and the White Christian experience is a blessing to the entire body of Christ, whether people of color see it that way or not. The era of Black Lives Matter is an opportunity for the entire body of Christ to learn and grow from the Black Christian experience.

What COVID-19 Exposed

The pandemic that impacted millions and took the lives of hundreds of thousands in 2020 did not keep people from going into the streets to protest injustice. It did not bring civility to or suspend a presidential election. It did not stop big-time collegiate and professional sports from crowning champions. It also did not bring people together. Instead, COVID-19 exposed the worst of many people. Militia groups invaded government buildings, angry individuals who felt their rights were being infringed on went into stores and restaurants refusing to wear masks, and politicians blamed the opposing party for the extent of the crisis.

But what about the Christian church? For many Christians, there was a frightening feeling that though the world was marching on in some ways, the church was closed. COVID-19 was able to halt the most visible expression of what it means to be church: the experience of worship within a building. Though many churches transitioned to online weekend worship experiences and midweek teachings and connections, many attenders were panicked with the thought of not being able to "go to church." The pandemic exposed a spiritual fragility within the church of the United States. It exposed the reality that *the church in the United States is more addicted to going to church than being the church in a mission field of ongoing crisis.*

The pandemic also exposed the allegiances that distract the church from its real purpose. The church may proclaim its purposes as evangelism, discipleship, and local and global missions, but the crisis exposed ongoing allegiances to the structures and systems of this world that compromise the church's ability to function as a sneak preview of the Kingdom of God. The racial unrest that arose once again, in spite of a pandemic, exposed another weakness of the church: *The church of the United States still remains a majority homogenous or racially segregated church.* This impacts the ability of the church to serve as a transformative and reconciling force amid a significant portion of the nation hitting the streets demanding racial justice. This is especially a problem for the evangelical church.

Evangelicalism is not seen broadly as an innovator when it comes to diversity, multiethnicity, justice, and beloved community. How can this be, with what seems to be a commitment to multiethnic church planting and an embrace of racial reconciliation? The answer lies in a conflicting history within evangelicalism of seemingly making a commitment to reconciliation and justice while at the same time promoting and profiting from a White American conservative, nationalistic, and supremacist framework of Christianity. This Whiteness I am referring to goes beyond an individualistic understanding or identity based on the color of one's skin. Whiteness is a collective understanding that describes those moving from European immigrant status into the dominant culture within a racialized society. Some today who are the descendants of this journey may not even see themselves as White but simply as American. Yet, this Whiteness is real and shapes a social framework. This framework lifts up a mythology of White Christian innocence while presenting a revisionist motif which reduces the historic impact of colonialism, slavery, Jim Crow segregation, and the subordination of women.

Evangelicalism also has a history of doing ministry in a way that places individual or personal evangelism and discipleship above advancing the Kingdom of God toward both individual and systemic transformation. This is coupled with a social engagement limited to the issues of a prolife position (which is itself limited to issues pertaining to life in the womb); marriage between one man and one woman; a preservation of the current State of Israel; and maintaining a majority of politically conservative judges on the Supreme Court. The preservation of these values within evangelicalism becomes the major roadblock for greater missional credibility in the areas of justice and reconciliation. In their book *Divided by Faith: Evangelical Religion and the Problem of Race in America*, Christian sociologists Michael Emerson and Christian Smith present some of the problems evangelicalism has faced in this area in recent years and in a more distant past:

Because evangelicals view their primary task as evangelism and discipleship, they tend to avoid issues that hinder these activities. Thus, they are generally not counter-cultural. With some significant exceptions, they avoid "rocking the boat," and live within the confines of the larger culture. At times they have been able to call for and realize social change, but most typically their influence has been limited to alterations at the margins. So, despite having the subcultural tools to call for radical changes in race relations, they most consistently call for changes in persons that leave the dominant social structures, institutions, and culture intact. . . . Evangelicals usually fail to challenge the system not just out of concern for evangelism, but also because they support the American system and enjoy its fruits.[1]

Emerson and Smith reveal a juxtaposition when it comes to evangelicalism's journey with justice and reconciliation. There are two personalities within evangelicalism, or what Joseph Evans describes as a "double consciousness within Whiteness."[2] This is a White privileged version of the double consciousness that W. E. B. Du Bois speaks of in relation to African Americans[3]—a persistent pressure to live in the tension between two distinctly different realities, identities, and value systems.

This double consciousness is one manifestation of the

historic and present spiritual crisis impacting the mission of the church. This spiritual crisis at the same time provides an opportunity to rediscover who the church is to be. When surrounded by crisis, the church can reclaim the power, authority, and resilience of the church of the first century—which, though surrounded by crisis, could not be stopped in its mission and purpose. There is an opportunity to understand the sovereignty of God within social crisis and also to rediscover participation in the great commission, in spite of whatever social crisis occurs.

The great commission is the call on the church to make disciples of all nations. In 2 Corinthians 5, Paul calls on the members of the church to serve as ambassadors of reconciliation, carrying its message and embodying its ministry. This should inform how the church is able to march on and not be paralyzed amid either a virus-based or a racial-based pandemic. The church must find its identity outside of a transactional and building-dependent ecclesiology in order to move toward a more prophetic and apostolic ecclesiology of equipping and releasing cross-cultural, reconciling, justice-oriented disciple makers.

The Ongoing Experience of Black Bodies in the United States

As the COVID-19 pandemic began, many strategies emerged to support "shelter in place," an initial response to the pandemic calling for people to only leave their homes for essential needs and essential work. There were commercials, cable-news specials, and even social-media gatherings to encourage people to stay home as much as possible. One particular social-media initiative that caught my attention was the "Instagram parties" put on by hip-hop deejays such as Jazzy Jeff and D-Nice. Hundreds of thousands tuned in for these urban social-media nightclubs targeting the hip-hop community broadly and African Americans more specifically. In between rap and R&B hits from the 1980s, 1990s, and 2000s, there were calls for African Americans and the broader urban community to stay safe and stay at home. Instead of considering social nightlife options in their surrounding community, the call was to party safely at home with people across the nation and world. But despite strategies to keep people safely at home when at all possible, systemic racism and racial disparities would show themselves as an ongoing social crisis, birthed even before the official founding of the United States of America.

The deaths of unarmed African Americans at the hands of police and self-deputized vigilantes in the first few months of 2020 continued a tragic narrative that not only points back to Trayvon Martin in 2012 but at least all the way back to Emmett Till in the 1950s. This time names such as Ahmaud Arbery, Breonna Taylor, and George Floyd were making national news and would drastically change the landscape dominated by a virus. The eight-minute, forty-six-second video of George Floyd crying out for his life on the corner of 38th Street and Chicago Avenue in Minneapolis, Minnesota, had a significant impact on the nation and world. While bystanders recording this horrific scene cried out for Floyd's life, police officer Derek Chauvin refused to lift his knee and weight off Floyd's neck. I was even more personally grieved by this video because I grew up on the block where this tragedy took place.

The ongoing social virus of systemic racism reminds us that Black bodies have never been granted full and sustained humanity in the United States of America. Black bodies have been relegated to slave bodies, treated as less than human. Slave bodies became whipped bodies, raped bodies, sold bodies, disposable bodies. Even after Black slave bodies were granted freedom, they eventually became terrorized bodies, lynched bodies, and segregated bodies within the system of Jim Crow. During the Civil Rights movement, Black bodies were beaten bodies during what would have been non-violent marches for equality. They were bombed bodies while in Sunday school. They were bodies bitten by police dogs and sprayed with the full force of fire hoses. They were assassinated bodies in a ballroom in New York or a hotel balcony in Memphis.

Black bodies are feared and have triggered White flight to flourishing suburbs on one hand, and the development of ghettos, project developments, and other forms of under-resourced communities on the other. And now, the twenty-first century has brought us graphic videos of the deaths of unarmed Black bodies at the hands of law enforcement: Stephon Clark, Eric Garner, Tamir Rice, and Alton Sterling, to name a few. This journey of the Black body in search of full humanity provides the framework for understanding the deaths of Ahmaud, Breonna, and George. Will the world ever see Black bodies as made in the image of God and meant by God to flourish, or will they always be seen as other than?

The marginalization of Black bodies is an experience of Black people in every sector of society. I am no idealist; I realize that none of the fallen systems and structures of this world will be fully redeemed and eternally transformed until Christ returns and makes everything right. But in the meantime, Christians can play a role in providing a sneak preview of what it looks like when the Kingdom of God comes to bear on unjust and broken systems, institutions, and structures. There is an opportunity amid social crisis for the church to show its true distinctiveness, to function as an embassy of the Kingdom of God. The church must be otherworldly in a world filled with crisis after crisis. It cannot afford to be held captive to the institutions, ideologies, systems, and structures of this world. When the church is more sold out to political parties, presidential candidates, nationalism, or race than identity in Christ and citizenship in the Kingdom of God, a spiritual crisis is exposed that hinders the mission of the church in the middle of social crisis.

The death of George Floyd both caused a reactionary disruption during the COVID-19 season and provided an opportunity for the church to discover a deeper understanding of the gospel and the Kingdom of God. That tragic moment launched two racialized floods that the coronavirus couldn't stop. One was protests. The hashtag and movement Black Lives Matter[4] once again flooded social media and cities, not only in Minneapolis, Chicago, and Los Angeles but also in London, Toronto, Sydney, Paris, and Tokyo. Also, in the US, there were protests in states where one might not expect them to take place, such as Montana, North Dakota, and South Dakota. A global pandemic could not stop a global call for justice and the cry that Black Lives Matter. Indeed, as millions around the world were testing positive for the coronavirus and hundreds of thousands were dying from it, the world was literally marching on. And these marches in the name of Black lives were multiethnic and multicultural like never before. It is especially important to note the number of young white men and women who took to the streets around the world.

A New Movement, a New Missional Opportunity

This Black Lives Matter movement can be seen as the Civil Rights movement of our day. There are so many similarities between the two movements:

- the deaths of unarmed African Americans by law enforcement and self-deputized vigilantes
- state laws that allow such treatment of Black bodies
- protests, marches, and rallies on the nation's Capitol
- unfortunate violent encounters between law enforcement and protesters

- conflicting strategies between nonviolent and violent expressions of resistance
- political polarization playing a major role in dividing the nation by race

But there is also a major difference between the Civil Rights movement and the Black Lives Matter movement: the involvement of the African American church.

There was no question that the most dominant expression of the Civil Rights movement was centered in the Black Church. Not only was Dr. Martin Luther King Jr. a key figure in the Civil Rights movement but so were ministers such as Ralph Abernathy, Fred Shuttlesworth, Jesse Jackson, and C. T. Vivian. The movement was also filled with Black Church laypeople like Fannie Lou Hamer and John Lewis. Nonviolent marches were preceded by rallies that took place within church sanctuaries. Trainings in nonviolent resistance were held in church fellowship halls and Sunday school classrooms. Prayers and hymns filled the air during marches and protests. Scriptural stories such as God hearing the cries of the oppressed in Egypt or opening the jail doors for Paul and Silas were utilized as biblical foundations to motivate participants.

Since the development and mainstream cultural entrance of the hip-hop movement, there has been a visible generation gap between the Black Church and the Black community. The hip-hop generation, the first generation after the Civil Rights movement era, is also the first generation to have a significant segment that didn't grow up in the Black Church. I would argue that the hip-hop generation and current subcultures, including hip-hop activism, hip-hop spirituality, and hip-hop politics, have more influence in the Black Lives Matter movement than the Black Church does.

Because the Black Lives Matter movement is not rooted in the Black Church in the same way as the Civil Rights movement was, there is a significant missional and mentoring opportunity for the Black Church—to inject biblical justice, reconciliation, and righteousness into the movement. More importantly, there are evangelism and disciple-making opportunities. The flourishing future of the Black Church and the African American–led multiethnic church resides in this movement. The Black Church has an opportunity to reclaim a missional heritage and connect more deeply to a contextualized ecclesiology.

In his book *A Black Political Theology*, J. Deotis Roberts contends that the liberation of the oppressed is the God-given mission of the Black Church.[5] He also assumes the incorporation of reconciliation in Black theology by seeing no separation between the liberating of the oppressed and the good news of the gospel of Jesus Christ. He makes this point when he states the following about reconciliation and Black theology:

> The incorporation of reconciliation into a black theology needs no justification. Reconciliation is an integral part of the gospel. Reconciliation is the

very essence of the good news. God in Christ is reconciling in the world and Christians are called to be agents of this reconciling gospel. The "whole" gospel includes reconciliation. The revelation of God includes what "ought to be" and what "must be" as well as what "is." . . . Reconciliation in our social climate includes a "cross" for all Christians.[6]

Similarly, the incorporation of a Black political theology into the praxis of the reconciling church needs no justification. Roberts states that a Black political theology is concerned with the whole person. His approach to Black theology is both existential and political.[7] Ambassadors of reconciliation are to be concerned with the souls of people; this includes how they exist and identify themselves in a broken and sinful world. They are also to be concerned about the oppressive systems, structures, and policies which infringe on their existence. There is also an opportunity to be God's present vehicle of incarnation. Just as Christ came to set the captives free and proclaim good news to the poor, there is an opportunity to walk in solidarity with the marginalized and oppressed today. The Black Church can be a bridge over the troubled waters of this racialized flood.

But there is not only a missional opportunity for the Black Church; there's an ecclesiological opportunity as well. The Black Church has been a tremendous force of evangelism, discipleship, liberation, empowerment, and community development among Black people from slavery until now. There is an ongoing missional opportunity to engage hip-hop culture and the Black Lives Matter movement that can lead to a more flourishing future for the Black Church.

Because the Black Lives Matter movement is becoming more and more a multiethnic and multicultural movement, it fuels the opportunity as well for post-Black Churches—congregations that are African American led but also multiethnic, reconciling, while retaining an orientation toward justice.

Many of the intentionally multiethnic church-planting movements and initiatives are being led and resourced by predominately White denominations and church-planting associations. There is a need for church-planting associations, denominations, networks, and movements that are African American led and include the prioritizing of multiethnic church planting. Another significant part of the ecclesiological opportunity is being a gift to the broader body of Christ, specifically evangelicalism.

This points to the second racialized flood that arose in the midst of the COVID-19 crisis in response to the death of George Floyd: the flood of double consciousness.

The Double Consciousness of White Evangelicalism

After the death of George Floyd, a number of senior pastors from large, predominately White, evangelical megachurches made statements against systemic racism and in support of Black lives. It seemed that more notable evangelical pastors, denominational leaders, and parachurch executives than ever before used their influence to draw attention to racism and to providing a biblical path to unity, justice, and transformation. A number of online conferences, webinars, and sermon series focusing on race, racism, reconciliation, and justice showed up on the social-media pages of many well-known evangelical churches. There were calls from pastors to their congregations to become more aware of systemic racism and to assist in moving from being a nonracist church to being an antiracist one.

At the same time, there were also influential evangelical pastors and leaders using their voices to dehumanize those killed by police officers, criminalize protestors, and give full-throated support to law enforcement. The existence of any form of systemic racism was denied by a significant segment of evangelicalism. Instead of the deaths of unarmed African Americans leading to empathy and lament from this segment, there were accusations of socialism, Marxism, and liberal agendas to lead the church away from the gospel. This recent revealing of a spiritual double consciousness when it comes to dealing with race is not a new dilemma for evangelicalism.

In the United States of America, evangelicalism has always lived on both sides of the "race coin." Evangelicals have preached freedom in Christ and supported slavery, have presented the Good News and the Kingdom of God and supported Jim Crow segregation, have promoted racial reconciliation and multiethnic church planting and played a significant role in the election of a towering and polarizing figure of racial division. With this history and present reality in mind, it should not be surprising to see such a reactionary response to the crying out of Black Lives Matter and the crying for justice, reconciliation, and transformation.

Systemic racism and political captivity are an ongoing crisis, and a segment of evangelicalism has been complicit. But there is a transformative opportunity for evangelicalism to missionally become a more multiethnic, reconciling, and liberating movement. By embracing an ecclesiological praxis of reconciliation, evangelicalism can develop greater credibility as a spiritually and socially transformative movement amid racialized crisis.

Reconciliation is the discipling and spiritual maturing work of God in the Holy Spirit and the restorative work of God embodied in the people of the church. Theologians Curtiss Paul DeYoung and Samuel Hines contend that reconciliation is God's one-item agenda, the work of God on the whole person and across the whole community. They challenge the church to put reconciliation at the forefront of their missional ecclesiology:

> Reconciliation with God and each other through
> Christ is the number one item on God's agenda.
> Oneness must be realized in the midst of an
> environment prone to alienation and polarization. . . .
> Reconciliation brings about peace, both between
> human beings and God and between individual

persons. In spite of all the efforts we make to come together, barriers exist and keep driving us apart. God conceived of reconciliation before the formation of the world.[8]

In Christ, diverse yet divided humanity is reconciled to God and reconciled to one another. The church, as a collection of the reconciled, is given the message and mission of reconciliation. God's agenda becomes the church's agenda and informs all areas of ministry life. As those having been reconciled to God through Christ, we become vehicles of reconciliation in a socially divided and unjust mission field.

One of the ways evangelicalism can gain a reconciling and justice-oriented ministry praxis is through the contextualized ecclesiology of the Black Church.

The Gifts of the Black Church to Evangelicalism

The missional and fruitful future of the evangelical church could hinge on its ability to humbly learn from Black ecclesiology and missiology.

The first gift of the Black Church is the gift of *missional liberation*. The Black Church was born within slavery in the United States of America. From its beginning, therefore, the Black Church had a holistic understanding of liberation in Christ. Liberation took on both physical and spiritual dimensions. One example of this is the ministry and social praxis of Harriet Tubman. As the "General" of the Underground

Railroad, Tubman did not separate her belief in Christ from her determination to set the captives physically free. The Black Church as an invisible church during slavery found a distinctive ecclesiology in the liberation story found in the book of Exodus.

The second gift is the gift of *sin understanding*. The Black Church understands that sin is housed in both the souls of human beings and in the structures, institutions, systems, and ideologies of society. Biblically, sin was not just housed in the soul of Cain, which led him to kill his own brother, Abel, but sin was also housed systemically in the empires of Egypt, Assyria, Babylon, and the Roman Empire. Systemic sin also showed up in the nation of Israel, the people with whom God made a covenant and to whom he promised a Messiah. Systemic sin in the form of idolatry and the mistreatment of the poor, the foreigner, the orphan, and the widow led to Israel becoming a divided nation and the experience of living collectively as the exiled and the oppressed. The Black Church sees bringing the Kingdom of God to bear on unjust systems and structures in a sinful world as part of its work.

The third gift of the Black Church is the gift of *justice orientation*. The Black Church sees justice as profoundly biblical. The Black Church understands the connection between justice and righteousness. Reconciliation and restorative justice are also deeply intertwined. To be reconciled to God through Jesus Christ is also to become connected back to God's mission for justice in a sinful world. The Black Church is concerned about the lost souls of human beings and about the systems, institutions, and structures that oppress and fail them.

◆　　◆　　◆

Regardless of the seasons of crisis that we unfortunately experience, the church must understand its true marching orders. The church is God's frontline vehicle for the gospel to invade souls and for justice to invade society in some visibly transformative way. In 2 Corinthians 5, Paul calls the church to the ministry and message of reconciliation. He presents Christ followers as ambassadors of reconciliation. In seasons of crisis, this should be the primary posture of the church. The church cannot afford to be mistakenly understood as finding its identity primarily in nationalism, political polarization, or hiding behind church walls as some form of a religious country club. The church must find its identity in its citizenship in the Kingdom of God. We must march forward as an army of cross-cultural, reconciling, justice-oriented disciple makers.

4

A BRIEF HISTORY
OF CRISIS

Marshall Shelley

From the beginning, Christians have known crisis. As Bruce Shelley begins his classic text, *Church History in Plain Language*, "Christianity is the only major religion to have as its central event the humiliation of its God."[1]

Yes, the flogging, stripping, shaming, agonizing, and very public crucifixion of the one called Emmanuel, "God with us," makes Christians a people familiar with crisis! Ever since, Christians look to that event whenever crises of other kinds arise, trusting that God will produce another act, if not of resurrection, at least of redemption and surprising regeneration of some sort.

But the record shows that when crises arise, Christians

are given to fear as well as faith. The temptation to respond to crisis with anger, scapegoating, desperation, and violence often overtakes some believers, even as others are able to view the crisis as an opportunity to demonstrate the vitality of faith, hope, and love.

The types of crises that Christians have encountered throughout history are many. Here are just a few examples:

The death of the Messiah. This was followed by his resurrection and ascension, leaving his followers to spread the gospel, led by the Spirit, apart from the visible presence of Christ. As the book of Acts and the Epistles point out, this transition and his followers' progress wasn't always smooth.

The destruction of Jerusalem and the Temple. When Roman legions put down a regional rebellion in AD 70, the center of worship for Jews (and the first Christians) was suddenly gone. This contributed to the dispersion, spread, and fragmentation of the Christian faith to Europe, Africa, Asia, even India, which eventually led to regional distinctives (Nestorian churches in the East, Mar Thoma churches in India, the Coptic Church in Egypt and Ethiopia) that some considered heretical.

Persecution, often severe. Periodically Christians were targeted within the Roman Empire as disloyal to Rome unless they proclaimed Caesar as Lord. Some Christians boldly maintained their faith unto death. Others succumbed to the pressure of torture and threat of death and "lapsed" from their faith, creating a crisis for the church, when the persecution subsided, of what to do when these "lapsed" members wanted to rejoin the church.

Abrupt identity crisis. When Christianity suddenly became the religion of Roman emperors after AD 312, the persecuted Christian minority quickly encountered the privileges and responsibilities and temptations and conflicts and failures that public influence brings. How does Christian faith, originally birthed among the marginalized, inform the stewardship of earthly power suddenly given to Christians? How would Christians treat the minority religions (and Christian dissidents) under their newly granted authority?

The shocking fall of Rome. In AD 410, the "Eternal City" was pillaged by Germanic barbarians. The collapse of the city considered the center of the visible church shook Christians' understanding of God's will and their place in the world.

Wars that periodically spanned the known world. These included the Crusades against Muslims (1096–1271), the Hundred Years' War (1337–1453, between England and France, both ostensibly Christian nations), the Thirty Years' War (1618–1648, which resulted in the deaths of more than eight million people, including 20 percent of the German population, one of the most destructive conflicts ever), and more recently, two twentieth-century world wars, the Cold War with the threat of nuclear annihilation, and countless regional conflicts that threatened to explode more widely. Christians were divided not only by wars but in their responses to those wars.

Highly contagious diseases. These included the Black Death (1346–1353, with recurring flare-ups afterward), smallpox, AIDS, and the global pandemic of COVID beginning in 2019. The responses of Christians to each of these dread diseases were not uniform, ranging from defensive and judgmental to compassionate and selfless.

While we can't develop the lessons from all seven of these types of crises here, we will take a deeper look at three historical crises to help us understand how Christians respond to crisis—and how crisis tests, reveals, and refines the faith of Christians.

The Fall of Rome: Searching for a Surer Foundation

For 620 years, since the days of Hannibal and his battle elephants, Rome had not faced an invading army. But in AD 410, Alaric, a Visigoth from northern Europe with a barbarian army, besieged the city.

A delegation from Rome went outside the walls to ask Alaric for his terms and to beg for mercy. Alaric's response:

"All your gold, all your silver, and all your German slaves!" The Romans stalled at these demands, even as conditions in the city deteriorated.

Finally Alaric's forces broke into and plundered the city, building by building. There was destruction everywhere— except in the churches. Alaric considered himself a Christian (the Roman church considered him a heretic, an Arian who wrongly defined the relationship between God the Father and Christ the Son). Despite the theological differences, Alaric restricted his troops from plundering the Roman churches. But the rest of the city was stripped of its valuables.

When the Visigoths left Rome, Christians the world over were stunned and confused. Rome, the epicenter of the Christian church, had fallen. "My voice sticks in my throat," wrote Jerome, echoing the feelings of all in the Roman Empire, Christian and pagan alike. "The City that took the whole world captive is itself taken."[2] The pagans, meanwhile, wondered if the traditional Roman gods could have saved the city. Were they angry because recent emperors had turned to the Christian God?

Refugees from Rome fled in all directions, many to the North African seaport of Hippo. The bishop there, Aurelius Augustine, heard their questions, their doubts. He realized someone needed to address the question: Where is God when what we believed was secure, even divinely blessed, is conquered? So Augustine began to write: Why had Rome fallen? Would the ruin of the Eternal City mean the collapse of Christianity? Was God also defeated?

Augustine's answers provided light not only for the dark days of the moment but a philosophy and a perspective that continues to this day whenever crisis hits.

Augustine compared the defeat of Rome with the judgment of Sodom. There had been a great deal of destruction, but cities, he said, consist of people, not buildings. Unlike Sodom, Rome had been chastised but not destroyed. Then he made a key distinction between two cities: the Worldly City, which inevitably rises and falls, and the heavenly City of God, which is everlasting. Earthly influence is not to be confused with eternal glory. These writings, which became his massive book *The City of God*, influence Christian thought even now.

The Worldly City, said Augustine, is united by desire for earthly things. The City of God is held together by the love of God. The Romans were driven to their great achievements by the pursuit of earthly glory. By contrast, "The Heavenly City outshines Rome, beyond comparison. There, instead of victory, is truth; instead of high rank, holiness; instead of peace, felicity; instead of life, eternity."[3]

And what about the church and the state? Augustine believed the church to be the only human community that worked to advance the City of God. The state had its role in suppressing crime and preserving peace, but, Augustine insisted, the state must defer to the Christian church and its higher, eternal values.

Augustine not only helped Christians of the fifth century regain equilibrium after the fall of Rome but his writings provided a foundation for the Holy Roman Empire and throughout the Middle Ages. In crises ever since, Christians have sought a higher view. The present might be bad, but God is on the throne, and a better world is in store. The golden age—the Kingdom of God—is in the future, not in the fading and vulnerable splendors of a temporary, worldly kingdom.

The Black Death:
Self-Preservation at What Price?

In 1347, according to writer Charles L. Mee Jr., "in all likelihood, a flea riding on the hide of a black rat [on a ship] entered the Italian port of Messina. . . . The flea had a gut full of the bacillus Yersinia pestis."[4] With that rat, flea, and bacillus came the most feared plague on record. Between 1347 and 1353, the Black Death killed more than one-third of the entire population in Eurasia and North Africa, easily over 20 million people.

The symptoms were gruesome: black swellings the size of eggs in armpits and groins, swellings that oozed blood and pus, and spreading boils and black blotches on the skin. The sick endured severe pain and died within five days of the first symptoms. According to the BBC's HistoryExtra.com, one observer noted: "The living were scarcely sufficient to bury the dead."[5]

As in most of the crises throughout history, some Christians responded well; others did not. Some obeyed Christ's command to "love one another." Others forsook that command in desperate pursuit of self-preservation. One Sicilian friar reported, "Magistrates and notaries refused to come and make the wills of the dying," and "even the priests did not come to hear their confessions."[6] In one account called the *Decameron*, the author wrote,

> Brother was forsaken by brother, oftentimes husband
> by wife; nay, what is more, and scarcely to be believed,
> fathers and mothers were found to abandon their own
> children to their fate, untended, unvisited as if they
> had been strangers.[7]

During the horror, many faithful priests, nuns, and friars bravely ministered to the sick and the dying. But attrition among them was severe. While 30 percent of the general population died, between 45 and 50 percent of priests died. One of the highest rates of mortality among priests was in the diocese of Manlake, where it reached 61 percent.[8]

According to one French chronicler, the nuns at one city hospital, "having no fear of death, tended the sick with all sweetness and humility." New nuns replaced those who died, until most had died: "Many times renewed by death, [they] now rest in peace with Christ as we may piously believe."[9] Philip Ziegler, in his book *The Black Death*, writes,

> The abrupt disappearance of nearly half the clergy,
> including a disproportionately great number of the
> brave and diligent, inevitably put a heavy strain
> on the machinery of the Church and reduced its

capacity to deal effectively with movements of protest or revolt.[10]

Christians' temptation to protest and revolt can take some ugly forms. Raymond Crawfurd, in *Plague and Pestilence in Literature and Art*, writes:

> Amid all the panic of the Black Death, persecution of the Jews broke out with even greater ferocity than during the Crusades. . . . Some victim was needed to appease the maddened populace: so the Jews were accused of poisoning the wells, and even of infecting the air . . . of secret operations directed from Toledo.[11]

Writing about Christian persecution of Jewish people during the Black Death, Mark Galli explains the brutal tactics:

> Lynchings began in the spring of 1348 following the first plague deaths. In France, Jews were dragged from their houses and thrown into bonfires.
>
> Pope Clement VI tried to stop the hysteria. He said Christians who imputed the pestilence to the Jews had been "seduced by that liar, the Devil," and that . . . the massacres were a "horrible thing." He urged priests to take Jews under their protection as he himself offered to do, but his voice was hardly heard in the rush to find a scapegoat.[12]

A second response was public gatherings of conspicuous piety. Assuming the plague was sent by God as a punishment, the only way to end it, Christians concluded, was repentance of sin and recommitment to God, the more public the better. So processions were organized, winding their way through towns to the church. Participants would fast, pray, parade, and purchase charms to keep them safe.

The Flagellant movement took this impulse further. These were zealous Christians, led by a Master, who roamed from town to city to countryside, gathering crowds and whipping themselves for their sins, criticizing the church for being ineffective, and stirring the persecution and killing of unbelievers: Jews, Roma, and other minority groups. Eventually church and state got the upper hand when Clement VI called for their arrest. "The flagellants disbanded and fled, 'vanishing as suddenly as they had come,' wrote [one witness], 'like night phantoms or mocking ghosts.'"[13]

By contrast, other Christians found solace amid the terrors of the plague in the presence of Christ. Julian of Norwich, England, was one example. She recorded experiences of her own sickness and survival and her mystical encounter with Jesus, writing both immediately afterward and after twenty years of contemplation. (She is thought to be the first woman to have written in English.) Some of her expressions are well known: "All shall be well, and all manner of things shall be well" (in *Revelations of Divine Love*).[14] No trite platitude, her statement was a product of suffering, a vision, and years of prayerful reflection.

Amid crises, including plague, suffering, and death, how does God want Christians to respond? For Julian, the answer was clear: "God always wants us to be secure in love, and peaceful and restful, as he is towards us."[15]

If only that were true of more Christians in times of crisis.

The 9/11 Terrorist Attacks: Short-Term and Long-Term Effects

Anyone born before 1990 remembers where they were on September 11, 2001. The attacks on the World Trade Center, the Pentagon, and the thwarted attack on the US Capitol shook the entire world. In the weeks afterward, great attention was given to prayer.

A chaplain with the American Red Cross's Spiritual Care Response Team at the World Trade Center site in New York remembers:

> It was Sunday evening when a firefighter came to me there in a panic and said, "Chaplain, I don't think I'm gonna make it to Mass today!" . . . St. Patrick's was the only [church] with an evening Mass and it was simply too far away.
>
> I invited him to join me in the cafeteria at a table beside the comfort dogs and stacks of cards from children everywhere. I asked him if he knew how many Masses were being celebrated around the world every day? He replied that he did not, and I said, "I think it's like over 300,000 masses every

day." And I asked him, "What do you think is on the minds of every person who went to Mass today?" He said, "The people and families lost here in this tragedy?" I said, "Yes! And where do you think they would want to be if they were able to?" He said, "Right here!" And I continued, "If we are truly a community of faith, then you need to let them be the ones who attend Mass for you today, and you need to be the one who stands here on their behalf. Does that make sense?" I asked, and he agreed that it did. And we finished our soup and bread and I don't think I ever saw him again.[16]

That spirit was widespread.

The Sunday following 9/11, churches "overflowed with distraught visitors."[17] At Redeemer Presbyterian Church in Manhattan, for example, normal attendance almost doubled, from 2,800 to nearly 5,400.

Pastor Tim Keller spoke from 1 Thessalonians 4:13, where Paul tells believers to grieve but "not like those without hope," and from John 11:20-53, where Jesus gave Lazarus new life. One member of Keller's church said, "The morning service that Sunday was so full that [Keller] said, 'Come back and we'll do another service right after this one,' . . . Just like that Redeemer grew another service."[18]

Churches everywhere in the city saw new faces on September 16. Lots of them. One report showed

that 40 percent of the evangelical churches in
New York as of December 2010 started since
2000.[19] Only an estimated 3 percent of New York's
residents attend an evangelical church. Still, that
figure has tripled since 1990. . . . The aftermath
of 9/11 was a growth spurt for evangelicals in
America's largest city.[20]

Even beyond New York, the terrorist attacks brought millions to prayer. But the longer-term effect wasn't quite as dramatic. Research indicated that in the two or three Sundays right after 9/11, 48 percent of respondents said that they had attended church that week. In subsequent weeks, the number returned to what it had been before the attacks, ranging from 25 to 40 percent, depending on the region.

Mark Chaves, professor of sociology and divinity at Duke University and director of the National Congregations Study, noted that the post-9/11 spike in church attendance did not last. "People thought this type of crisis . . . would lead people to be more religious, and it did," he says. "But it was very short-lived. There was a blip in church attendance and then it went back to normal."[21]

Perhaps part of the reason was that national leaders were encouraging people to return to "normal life" because if they didn't, "the terrorists have won."

So to the dismay of some church leaders, the call of the nation's leaders was not to prayer, greater trust in God, or service to others. Instead, it was "don't let the terrorists win;

get back to shopping, traveling, schooling, and life as normal." And "normal" soon included a global war on terror that involved military action in Afghanistan and soon spread to Iraq, Syria, and other parts of the region. That war was still being fought almost twenty years later.

On the other hand, living a "normal" Christian life is seen by other believers as the right and faithful response to crisis. They suggest that crisis should not call Christians to do anything other than what they're called to do all the time. Vernon Grounds wrote a few weeks after the attacks:

We who are Christians share with all our fellow Americans the shock, the grief, the anger, the pain, and even the fear aroused by that ghastly deed. And yet as Christians, while we react as ordinary human beings, our perspective is modified by our faith in the wisdom, love, and sovereignty of God. While we realize the truth of Proverbs 27:1, it's impossible to "know what a day may bring forth," we can and do commit each day's happenings into the almighty hands of our heavenly Father.[22]

He quoted a prayer of Robert Louis Stevenson, best known as the author of *Treasure Island*, that he taught to his family. It included this petition:

When the day returns, call us up with morning faces and morning hearts, eager to labor, happy if

happiness be our portion, and if the day be marked
for sorrow, strong to endure.[23]

During a crisis, Christians are called to do what they're always
supposed to do. Faithful living is just more conspicuous in
a crisis.

The Enduring Themes

This quick overview of the history of Christians' experience
over two millennia of culturally disruptive and protracted
crises suggests several themes.

Crisis is a testing of faith. The apostle Peter, writing to
Christians who were enduring crises of persecution and suffering, put it this way:

> For a little while you may have had to suffer grief
> in all kinds of trials. These have come so that the
> proven genuineness of your faith—of greater worth
> than gold, which perishes even though refined by
> fire—may result in praise, glory and honor when
> Jesus Christ is revealed.
>
> I PETER 1:6-7

Without crisis of some sort, faith may be genuine, but its
genuineness is not outwardly seen. A person's embodiment
of faith amid crisis is more evident and will result in praise,
glory, and honor when Jesus returns. The time of crisis is
simply a more visible context in which faith is to be lived out.

Of death, be not afraid. Personal mortality is one crisis that everyone will experience. Being able to trust God in the face of it is a test of faith for all. John Wesley was an example of steadfast faith in a Savior and Redeemer. A woman once asked Wesley, "Supposing that you knew you were to die at twelve o'clock to-morrow night, how would you spend the intervening time?" Wesley's reply was:

How, madam? Why, just as I intend to spend it now. I should preach this evening at Gloucester, and again at five to-morrow morning. After that I should ride to Tewkesbury, preach in the afternoon, and meet the societies in the evening. I should then repair to friend Martin's house, who expects to entertain me, converse and pray with the family as usual; retire to my room at ten o'clock, commend myself to my heavenly Father, lie down to rest, and wake up in glory.[24]

That's the posture of faith amid crisis. Whether facing global conflict or personal mortality, the calling of a Christian is to live with faith, hope, and love.

Look for God's sovereign and redemptive purposes. In any crisis, faith means looking for—and praying for—God to bring good out of crisis. Billy Graham, the twentieth-century evangelist who preached the gospel to more people worldwide than anyone before in history, was known for his simple, clear, and direct presentation. He essentially had only one sermon outline that he used over and over and over. It drew on and addressed the reality of crises in this world—a reality that has existed throughout human history.

1. The world is broken (evidenced by, pick one: war, racism, oppression, natural disasters, crisis of another sort . . .).
2. Jesus is the answer to the brokenness of human existence.
3. Won't you receive Jesus?

In a TED talk he gave in 1998, his outline was on full display.[25] To a crowd of technology and culture makers, he started with a couple of self-effacing introductory stories before he presented his points:

1. There are three things that technology, as wonderful and amazing as it is, cannot fix: (a) human evil; (b) human suffering; and (c) death.
2. Jesus came to address these enduring and inescapable realities.
3. I encourage you to put your faith in Jesus.

Throughout history, this has been the foundational response of Christians to crises large and small. Christians are not immune to crisis, but neither are Christians abandoned to crisis. Christians are called to demonstrate faith amid whatever the current crisis happens to be, to look to the resurrection of Jesus as their hope, and to respond to those around them with love. Easy? No. Proof of the genuineness of their faith? Yes.

5

THE BIBLE'S
CATALOG OF CRISIS

Sean Gladding

By the rivers of Babylon we sat and wept
when we remembered Zion.
There on the poplars
we hung our harps,
for there our captors asked us for songs,
our tormentors demanded songs of joy;
they said, "Sing us one of the songs of Zion!"
How can we sing the songs of the LORD
while in a foreign land?

PSALM 137:1-4

THE KINGDOM CONVERSATIONS SERIES is rooted in the recognition that those seeking to follow Jesus must be conscious of and respond to three realities at once: the past, the present, and the future. This chapter is concerned with the *past*. What can we learn from the people of God whose stories are told in the Hebrew Bible? And as this volume in the series is concerned with what we can learn from our ancestors during times of crisis, it seems pertinent to focus on the greatest crisis we find in the pages of those Scriptures: the Babylonian exile.

There really is no way to overstate the catastrophe that

the Babylonian exile was for God's people, nor the crisis with which it presented them. Forced migration has been a persistent tragedy of history, and it was experienced as just that by the former residents of Jerusalem and Judah who made the long journey from Ramah to Babylon in the sixth century BC (Jeremiah 40:1). They were not merely being deprived of their homeland—they were being stripped of everything that gave them their identity, provoking a theological crisis. It's not difficult to imagine the kinds of conversations that took place as they trudged the dusty road to Babylon.

> If the LORD is the one, true God, then how have
> the Babylonians defeated us? Did not God promise
> this land to our ancestors Abraham, Isaac, and Jacob
> and to us, their descendants? How is it possible that
> we are being forced to leave? Did not God make a
> covenant with us at Mount Sinai, after freeing us
> from slavery in Egypt? Did Solomon not build a
> great House for the Lord, a Temple that has now
> been desecrated, its furnishings stripped and carried
> off? Has not God loved us with an everlasting love?
> Has God now forgotten us? Has God abandoned us?
> What will happen to us now?

What do you do when everything that gives you your identity is stripped away?

I'm writing this chapter while seated in my favorite neighborhood coffee shop. Normally it would be packed with the lunch-hour crowd, the volume loud, peoples' names being called from the counter, orders ready to be picked up. Peals of laughter would ring out occasionally as friends caught up, business deals were struck, and college students enjoyed a break between classes. Elbows would rub, chairs would be bumped as people made their way between tables balancing a Third Street Club sandwich in one hand and an Angela Davis latte in the other. But today there are just a handful of people sitting at some of the half-dozen tables, plenty of distance between us, masks being pulled down and up as we sip our beverage of choice. The COVID-19 pandemic has drastically changed our lives, a global crisis that has changed how we work, how we educate, how we socialize, how we exercise, how we shop. And how we worship.

Many congregations are still not gathering for corporate worship in person, six months after we first closed the doors to our sanctuaries. Some were prepared to shift Sunday worship entirely online; many were not. Overnight, pastors had to open Zoom Pro accounts, learn how to stream live on Facebook, buy tripods for their phones to record sermons at home, discover what "Mbps" means, and find answers to a myriad of other technological questions. Church members found ourselves watching worship from the couch, some of us in our pj's. Small groups grew even smaller, and we had to find new places to meet (if at all). Many of our service opportunities were no longer possible, and we missed the sense of connection and purpose they provided.

Even for those congregations who chose to resume

in-person worship services, they were often a far cry from what we were used to: struggling to figure out who that masked person was waving at us from across the aisle; not being able to sit in "our" seat because that pew was roped off; missing older members who didn't feel safe coming back yet; no singing, no choir; no hugs; and no sharing from the common loaf and cup, if Communion was celebrated at all. We may have been glad to be back in the building, but it was not what we remembered. Not what we needed.

We wept when we remembered Zion.

◆　◆　◆

Crises can generally be divided into two categories: those that happen *to* us, and those that happen *because of* us. But it's also true that—more often than we like to admit—we confuse the two. Either through denial or a failure to see cause and effect, we are often the cause of crises we believe originated outside of ourselves. Years (if not decades) of deferred maintenance can often create crises for congregations, but it's easier to blame the storm that flooded the education wing than it is to acknowledge the lack of attention we'd paid to the condition of our building. We have asked way too much of our Sunday worship services and our paid leadership in terms of our formation in the Way of Jesus, and many of us— especially those with young children and youth—discovered we were ill-equipped to nurture our faith and faithfulness without the building.

This was certainly the case for Judah in the sixth century BC. While it may have been the Babylonians who carried them off into exile, Judah was largely responsible for what happened. The roots of their catastrophe go back centuries, to another crisis in Israel's story.

Without question, the "Golden Era" of Israel's history was during the reign of its third king, Solomon. Following the disastrous reign of Saul and the struggle to unite the northern and southern tribes during David's reign, Israel experienced an unparalleled time of peace and prosperity under Solomon. But the movement of God that began in the wilderness ground to a halt with the building of a great Temple in Jerusalem. This was not at God's request (see 2 Samuel 7). God had guided the steps of Israel through the movement of the Tabernacle, which they had followed. But with the building of a Temple, a new era began: one of static religion. A movement became an institution, and one which God's prophets would critique vociferously over the following centuries.

Solomon's son Rehoboam failed to maintain the tenuous unity of the twelve tribes, and in doing so sparked centuries of civil war. The ten northern tribes of Israel would eventually be taken into exile by the Assyrians, leaving the tribe of Judah as the sole surviving remnant of Abraham's descendants living in the land that God had promised him. But they didn't learn from the cautionary tale that the fate of their brother tribes provided, and the final kings of Judah were only capable of delaying their inevitable conquest by Babylon.

And then came the catastrophe of exile.

◆   ◆   ◆

Let's rejoin those people gathered by the river—either the Tigris or the Euphrates—where unplayed harps are hung on willows, while those who brought them into exile make fun of them, tormenting them. The humiliations pile on. Strangers in a strange land: ziggurats atop mountains, not Solomon's Temple; hanging gardens instead of olive groves; your nobility serving the emperor who dragged you from the Promised Land. And where is God in all this?

You may be familiar with Psalm 137 thanks to the musical *Godspell*. Or, if you lived in the UK during the 1970s, through the music of Boney M. (I love both versions). But even if that's the case, most of us probably can't recite the conclusion of the psalm from memory:

> Daughter Babylon, doomed to destruction,
>   happy is the one who repays you
>   according to what you have done to us.
> Happy is the one who seizes your infants
>   and dashes them against the rocks.
>
> PSALM 137:8-9

The rawness of the psalmist's words indicates the depth of pain the Exile caused the people of Judah. And they reveal what we have already noted: When we experience a crisis, we typically see it as something that is happening *to* us, rather than something *we* have caused. Yes, it was the Babylonians who conquered Judah and carried its people into exile, but the prophets had given the leaders of Judah ample warning that this was a fate they could avoid, if they changed the way they lived. But the kings and others with power ignored the prophets. The miserable record of this can be found in the definitive litany of the books of the Kings: "And [this king] did evil in the sight of the LORD, according to all his fathers had done." Having watched their brother tribes to the north being carried into exile by the Assyrian empire; having had to pay tribute to Egypt after Pharaoh Neco imprisoned King Jehoahaz; having watched helplessly as the Babylonians looted the Temple and carried off the first wave of Judaeans into exile—even then, Judah's leadership continued to turn to their idols instead of to the Living God for deliverance.

The idolatry of the kings went hand in hand with their failure to care for their people. Jehoahaz's successor, King Jehoiakim, taxed his people to pay tribute to Egypt, even as he built a luxurious palace for himself in Jerusalem (2 Kings 23:35; Jeremiah 22:13-14). This continued the pattern of his predecessors, whose oppression of their own people consistently came under condemnation by the prophets.

It's important to understand this history if we are to learn from our ancestors' experiences—especially their mistakes. The crisis of the Babylonian exile presented God's people with an opportunity to rethink everything—to reflect on their experience, to learn from the catalog of their forebears' mistakes and maybe *this* time choose to listen to the word of the Lord that came through the prophets while they were in exile, one of whom was Jeremiah.

If I were to ask you to quote one verse of Jeremiah from memory, chances are it would be this one:

"For I know the plans I have for you," declares the LORD, "plans to prosper you and not to harm you, plans to give you hope and a future."

JEREMIAH 29:11

You may well have a plaque hanging on a wall in your home somewhere with that verse written in decorative script. It's a text we like to offer to people as a comforting word in hard times, as an encouragement to keep going, to trust God. We may even know that these words are taken from a letter Jeremiah wrote to the people in exile in Babylon. But my guess is, if I asked you what precedes this beloved verse, those words may not spring so readily to mind.

Jeremiah's audience included the psalmist who wished violence on his captors' infant children. And while the people who found themselves in Babylon wept for their plight, the letter Jeremiah sent to them from Jerusalem was also tear-stained.[1] And this was the word of the Lord to the people in exile:

Build houses and live in them; and plant gardens and eat their produce. Take wives and become the fathers of sons and daughters, and take wives for your sons

and give your daughters to husbands, that they may
bear sons and daughters; and multiply there and do
not decrease.

JEREMIAH 29:5-6, NASB

God is telling the people of Judah that they are going to
be in exile for a long time (seventy years, in fact). There will
be no dramatic rescue this time. So, "settle down in Babylon.
Make a life for yourselves in exile." I'm sure when Jeremiah's
letter was read out to the assembly by the river, those words
provoked more weeping. But if that was painful to hear, what
followed would have provoked an outcry:

"And seek the welfare of the city where I have sent
you into exile, and pray to the LORD on its behalf;
for in its welfare lies your welfare."

JEREMIAH 29:7, ADAPTED FROM NASB

"Wait, what? Seek the welfare of our *enemies*? *Pray* for
them? I don't think so." It's not hard to imagine that kind
of response to Jeremiah's letter. The law may very well pre-
scribe loving your neighbors as yourself, but how can you
possibly do that when your neighbors are these wretched
Babylonians? How indeed.

I'm not really one for "life verses," but if I had to choose
one, it would be Jeremiah 29:7 (not verse 11). In fact, it was
one of the first Scriptures our children memorized with us.
It has become a guiding principle for how we live our lives,

and the key—for our family, at least—is the latter part of the verse: the recognition that our welfare is inextricably bound up with the welfare of our neighbors. As the people in exile wrestled with their identity, I wonder if they reconsidered the covenant God had made with their ancestor Abraham: "All peoples on earth will be blessed through you" (Genesis 12:3). But does that include Babylonians? If the greatest commandment is indeed to love God and to love your neighbor as yourselves (Mark 12:28-34), then to experience the kind of flourishing life for which God created us necessitates our willingness to both desire that same life for our neighbors and work together with them toward that end. Even if we don't like them. Even if we see them as enemies. This clearly flies in the face of the radically individualistic culture of the US, one which operates from a model of scarcity, in which there is *not* enough for everyone, so we have to get ours while we can, and protect it at all costs. Those are strong cultural currents, and it's hard to resist them. But crises often provide opportunities to do so.

In the seven years our family spent in Houston, we lived through three hurricanes, the last of which was Hurricane Ike in September 2008. Our home was without power for three weeks. The debris of downed trees was piled six feet high along the streets of our neighborhood. The heat and humidity of September in Houston is bad enough *with* electricity; without it, it was miserable. Yet, as soon as the storm passed, neighbors with generators were running extension cords across streets to enable others to keep their fridges and freezers going. People pulled grills out onto their driveways and began to cook food that was spoiling. Large groups of people gathered to share it, contributing what they could to these informal feasts. One neighbor brewed endless pots of coffee every morning, and many of us would gather to hang out, most of us unable to work because of the loss of power and/or streets being impassable. There was a remarkable spirit of togetherness as people who had lived on the same street for years—but who had never really met each other—began to share food and stories and grilling tips. I remember one neighbor saying, "It would be a real shame if we stopped doing this once life returns to normal. We should make plans to keep having coffee or cookouts together." And we all agreed. But when life did return to normal, we all got busy again, and those informal feasts and leisurely mornings over coffee came to a sudden end. Sure, we still waved to each other as we passed on the street, even calling people by name (having learned them). But the spirit of togetherness that the crisis had formed dissipated soon afterward.

And that's the problem with crises. They may bring out the best in us at the time, often giving us a taste of what life can be like when we recognize that we are—in fact—all in this together. They also provide an opportunity to step back and rethink everything. Why do we do what we do? Will what we're doing continue to serve us well into the future? But the desire for things to return to normal because of the challenges that crises present is so strong that when normal life does resume, we throw ourselves back into our familiar routines with a sigh of relief. We fail to build on our experience of togetherness for the long haul, and we fail to wrestle with crucial questions. As Seth Godin noted in his daily email on September 24, 2020, "This is precisely why normal is what normal is, because we fight to get back to it."[2]

Writing these words during the coronavirus pandemic of 2020—an extended crisis unlike any other in my lifetime—I can't help but wonder if things will be any different this time. Because, sadly, it seems instead of the sense of togetherness crises often bring, the pandemic has actually magnified our tendency toward selfishness and self-centeredness. There has been much more talk about "rights" than responsibilities, much less about "loving our neighbor as ourselves." But that was the word that came to the people in exile in Babylon, and it remains the great commandment, even during the crisis of a global pandemic.

Being asked to pray for your enemies and to seek their welfare is hard enough, but when those same enemies looted, burned, and destroyed the Temple that lay at the heart of your life, well, that's a whole other kind of ask. But the Temple was gone, and the rituals and rhythms that defined Israel's life had been stripped from them. It became obvious that there would be no return to normal any time soon. So how did the people adapt to this new reality? How could they maintain their identity as God's people?

It appears they settled on getting serious about the practice of Sabbath. To take one day in seven to rest from their work, a day to honor and delight in the Lord. This may have been in part because of the prophet who authored the latter part of the book of Isaiah, in which he urges the people to practice justice, and then God will respond to their plight. And then,

> "Your people will rebuild the ancient ruins
>   and will raise up the age-old foundations;
> you will be called Repairer of Broken Walls,
>   Restorer of Streets with Dwellings."
> ISAIAH 58:12

That was the hope of Israel in exile—the return and rebuilding of Jerusalem. But the prophet continues:

> "If you keep your feet from breaking the Sabbath
>   and from doing as you please on my holy day,
> if you call the Sabbath a delight
>   and the LORD's holy day honorable,
> and if you honor it by not going your own way
>   and not doing as you please or speaking idle words,
> then you will find your joy in the LORD,
>   and I will cause you to ride in triumph on the
>   heights of the land
>   and to feast on the inheritance of your father Jacob."
> ISAIAH 58:13-14

"Carry with you what you have learned in this crisis." And it appears the people listened. In fact, as many have observed down through the centuries, it was not so much that the Jews kept the Sabbath but that the Sabbath kept them. It was this practice that would come to define their identity, the one thing they would always be able to do, no matter their circumstances. When everything else was stripped away—as even a cursory glance at history shows has been the tragic experience of many of the descendants of those exiled in Babylon—the people still practiced Sabbath. Even when crammed into ghettos, or hiding in attics, or dying in concentration camps.

The COVID-19 pandemic has stripped away much of what the church has taken for granted. And the questions before us have been: *What gives us our identity? What will we do now in order to be faithful?* (Those are questions worth wrestling with even when we're not in the middle of a global pandemic.) If people asked you why they should consider your church, how would you respond? "You'll love the music! The preaching is great! We have a beautiful sanctuary! The teaching is biblical!" All of those may be true. But what do we do when we can't worship in our sanctuaries? Or hear the choir sing? Or the band play? Or sit in a packed Sunday school room? What then?

Before we rush to return to normal following a crisis, perhaps we should pause and ask what it means to return to our roots as a community that worships and serves the triune God. And, as I heard NPR journalist Michele Norris say on Michelle Obama's podcast, "Don't reach for normal . . . reach for better."[3] When the people did finally return to Jerusalem seventy years after being carried into exile, they clearly wanted a return to normal. And normal apparently meant a building: the Temple. Static religion. But when they laid the foundations for the new Temple, some of those who had wept by the rivers of Babylon—now old men—wept again, even as the younger generations cheered (Ezra 3:12-13). The prophet Haggai gave this word from the Lord:

> "Who is left among you who saw this temple in its former glory? And how do you see it now? Does it not seem to you like nothing in comparison?"
>
> HAGGAI 2:3, NASB

I wonder how many of the generation who built so many church buildings with large education wings across the United States now walk those often empty halls and wonder the same thing? I wonder how many of us will return to our church buildings after this pandemic runs its course, but without those who drifted away while it lasted, nor older members who will never feel safe enough to return? What will we have learned from this particular crisis? What can we learn from the example of God's people in exile in Babylon, who (re)discovered something new—the practice of Sabbath—as a way of maintaining a faithful identity when everything else had been stripped away? And what will we learn from the cautionary tale they provide in their longing for static religion, in the building of the Temple? Having lived through this profoundly challenging experience of trying to be the church without a building, many of us have discovered new ways to connect, worship, and serve in smaller settings outside of our "Temple." It has been challenging but at times exciting, providing glimpses of new possibilities. When the next crisis hits, will we know what to do in order to remain faithful?

Or will we just sit and weep when we remember Zion?

◆　　◆　　◆

If your experience of the crisis of the 2020 pandemic involved more grief than hope, then be encouraged by the Word that God spoke through the prophet Haggai to those old men weeping as they looked on the new Temple built in Jerusalem following the promised return from exile. For there is no question that we will continue to enter, walk through, and—God willing—come out the other side of crises, secure in our identity as the beloved of God, even as we continue to wrestle with what it means to be a faithful church.

> "But now take courage . . . ," declares the LORD,
> ". . . and work; for I am with you. . . . My Spirit is abiding in your midst; do not fear!"
> HAGGAI 2:4-5, NASB

6

JESUS WOULDN'T WASTE A CRISIS

Lee Eclov

AFTER HURRICANE KATRINA DEVASTATED NEW ORLEANS, one pastor told his decimated church, "We've always said that Jesus is all we need. Well, now Jesus is all we have." When the COVID-19 pandemic bullied its way into churches, all we had was Jesus. Our buildings sat empty. Our plans fizzled. Strategies stopped dead in their tracks. We couldn't even be together for Easter Sunday! We found ourselves unsure of how to do the most basic things—sing, preach a sermon, serve Communion, visit the sick, pray together, evangelize—never mind growing our churches or touting our worship services.

We still had Jesus, but we weren't sure of just what he had to say to us or what he wished us to do. At first, pastors preached about fear and God's protection. But after that, when we had to settle into a new reality, it was as if we'd awakened in a strange room at night, unsure of how to take a step without stubbing our toe. So what does it mean for Christians facing a catastrophic crisis to have nothing more than Jesus?

Survival Training

When Judas slipped away from that final Passover meal with Jesus to fulfill his diabolical contract, John added ominously, "And it was night" (John 13:30). The epic crisis was soon upon them. John 13–17 recounts how Jesus, in his final hours, prepared his disciples—all of us—for life without him in this dark world. The crisis ahead of them was not only that he would be gone but that they would face the world's hatred as surely as he had.

What Jesus taught his disciples that night prepares us not only for the hatred of the world but also for its catastrophes. Jesus' teaching in John 13–17 was new. While he had hinted at some of these themes before, what we learn here (now so familiar to us) was the capstone of Jesus' teaching. The rest wouldn't hold together without this. Every congregation worth its salt must know and embody what Jesus taught. Here is how we shine in this midnight world. Here is Christian survival training.

Significantly, Jesus' first lesson began with him taking the basin of water, laying aside his outer garments, slipping to his knees before his disciples, and washing their feet—even Judas's. "I have set you an example," he said, "that you should do as I have done for you" (John 13:15). Then, shortly after Judas left, Jesus made it clear: "Where I am going, you cannot come" (John 13:33). With that foreboding news hanging heavily upon them, Jesus gave them foot-washing instructions in triplicate: "A new command I give you: *Love one another*. As I have loved you, so you must *love one another*. By this everyone will know that you are my disciples, if you *love one another*" (John 13:34-35, emphasis added).

When the church faces the dark night of catastrophe, that is Rule #1: Get your basin and towel, get low, and love one another. Love the neighbors around you as God leads, but *always* "love one another." Pressure inevitably pulls at the seams of our relationships, so our love must be tightly woven before the night falls on us.

The disciples must have been reeling. Jesus was leaving them, and they couldn't follow. Jesus stunned them again when he said that the Rock among them would very shortly disown him three times (John 13:38). Then, in a response to their stunned silence, he said the most counterintuitive thing: "Do not let your hearts be troubled" (John 14:1).

Easier said than done, of course. Especially when our world is falling apart. Jesus' second coming somehow seems too far removed to be of much immediate consolation to believers swamped by crisis. Yet that is what Jesus offered the Eleven that dark night. As we'll see, Jesus often pointed his disciples to his return.

Christ's second coming reorients us to the fact that what we face now is not the end of the matter. This hope peels our white knuckles off our earthly securities. When we're glued to our TVs and news feeds, we forget to look up, forget that our redemption is drawing near. Our worship songs, our sermons, and our passing words of encouragement should often have a faraway look about them.

Greater Works

But what about life here and now, especially when calamity is crushing us? Jesus allows no one to cower in a corner. "Very truly I tell you, whoever believes in me will do the works I have been doing, and they will do even greater things than these, because I am going to the Father" (John 14:12). The astonishing spread of the gospel recorded in Acts is proof of Jesus' promise. The early church burgeoned under the pressure of persecution. So prepare the church to step into the mess! Run toward the trouble like David's mighty men.

And how will we as believers do the work of Christ if some cataclysm envelops us? Jesus has already told us that our first priority is to *humbly love and serve one another*. He's already told us to live on our toes for his return and everlasting days with him. Now, Jesus tells us how it is possible that we can do even greater works than he did when he walked the earth.

We must also pray with gutsy faith that *we would display the grace, truth, and loving unity of Jesus*. He said, "I will do whatever you ask in my name, so that the Father may be glorified in the Son. You may ask me for anything in my name, and I will do it" (John 14:13-14), an extravagant promise he repeated in John 15:7; 16:23, 26. Remember the powerful praying of the believers who were facing persecution in Acts 4:24-30. "Now, Lord, consider their threats and enable your servants to speak your word with great boldness. Stretch out your hand to heal and perform signs and wonders through the name of your holy servant Jesus" (verses 29-30). God did indeed give them boldness, and the miraculous sign they prayed for turned out to be not healings but astonishing Christian unity: "All the believers were one in heart and mind. No one claimed that any of their possessions was their own, but they shared everything they had" (Acts 4:32).

We, too, must come together as God's people to pray for boldness and supernatural evidence that Jesus is Lord. Especially in dark times! God waits for us to pray. I know that God's people are often more inclined to attend a church picnic than a prayer gathering. Nonetheless, we must persist, challenging our brothers and sisters over and over, if we must, to join us. Then, when we bow before the Lord, use Scripture for muscular language to lay claim to God's promises to supply any and every Kingdom resource we can imagine.

Continuing with Jesus' final instructions, *obey Christ's commands out of love for him.* Jesus said, "If you love me, keep my commands" (John 14:15). Jesus did not actually give us many commands, but those he did give, like "believe in me," "love one another," and "ask anything in my name," knead themselves into every aspect of life. Christlike thinking and behavior, fed by our love for him, shines brightest in a frightening darkness and sharpens people's taste for God when there is a spiritual famine in the land. Emergency workers often say how their training kicked in under pressure, enabling them to do what seems heroic. "I was just doing my job," they say. So it is with Christians under pressure who are already practiced in loving, trusting obedience.

Such obedience is to become, quite literally, second nature to us. That requires us to *rely on the Holy Spirit, whom Christ has sent to empower and educate us.* "I will ask the Father, and he will give you another advocate to help you and be with you forever—the Spirit of truth" (John 14:16-17), Jesus told his followers. Life in the Sprit is like walking on water. We can't really imagine doing it till we try, till we step out of the boat and onto the dark water. For example, we soon learn how daunting Jesus' command to love one another is. It's impossible, really, for who can generate the will or the wisdom to love a perplexing, disagreeable fellow believer? Such love is all the more difficult when our nerves are frayed and the world around us is tossing. Yet such is the buoying work of the Holy Spirit in our lives. When we cannot discern where to safely plant our feet, the Spirit leads us into and onto all truth.

A bit later, Jesus explained to us that the Holy Spirit not only works within our lives but also in proving "the world to be in the wrong about sin and righteousness and judgment" (see John 16:8-11). As C. S. Lewis said, God "shouts in our pain: it is His megaphone to rouse a deaf world."[1] The church can take heart that, thanks to the Holy Spirit, God is not silent when the world seems to be afire.

As Jesus led his disciples toward the garden of Gethsemane,

he laid out another essential of our faith, this also only possible through the Holy Spirit: *We must remain in Christ for life and fruit.* "As the Father has loved me, so have I loved you," he explained. "Now remain in my love. If you keep my commands, you will remain in my love" (John 15:9-10).

Recently our part of the country was hit by ferocious windstorms, even tornadoes, pounding down fields of corn, wheat, and soybeans. A farmer told me that only time would reveal whether his crop would stand back up or lie lifeless and fruitless. Calamities have that effect on our spiritual lives. They lay us low; they lay whole churches low. So spiritual leaders and other mature believers must strengthen our brothers and sisters by prayer, admonition, and practical graces.

All these are the building blocks of the ordinary Christian life, but they are also our unique survival tactics when the world seems to be coming apart at the seams. This is how Jesus prepared his disciples for the darkness ahead of them. Congregations schooled and practiced in these basics will be still standing when the storm has passed.

"All this I have told you," Jesus said in John 16:1, "so that you will not fall away." That is the danger facing Christians under pressure, individually and congregationally. Not that we'll be crushed but that we'll abandon Jesus. Crises lay open the hearts of our churches. God may not cause these upheavals, but he commandeers them for his purposes, exposing his glory through humble churches and revealing the emptiness of the world around us.

Unlike any crisis I've witnessed in my seventy years, the pandemic of 2020 laid bare the true health of churches, not evident by the typical measures of size, budgets, or programs but by holy resilience. We saw the fickleness of professing Christians, especially those who were churchless or merely churchy. Countless feckless attenders dropped away altogether or bounced from one video venue to another. But we also saw churches of no great reputation who proved to be faithful, loving, and hope-filled. For some, it was their finest hour.

The pastor said, "Now Jesus is all we have." Jesus said, in so many words, "This is what you have. Love one another with servant hearts. Rest assured that I will return for you. If you love me, obey me; and to make that possible, I'll send the Holy Spirit so that you can abide in me. And till I return, ask for anything—*anything*—you need to live for me in this troubled world."

Watch!

In her book *Eiffel's Tower*, Jill Jonnes tells about the fabulously wealthy American newspaper publisher, James Gordon Bennett, who lived in the late 1800s. He had two lavish apartments in Paris, plus a French country estate and a yacht harbored in Europe. He also had three homes in the US, even though he hadn't lived in the country for over ten years. She writes, "Each was fully staffed, ready to serve Bennett should he stride in the front door unannounced—the wine cellars were kept stocked, fires roared in the grates, and sheets were turned down nightly."[2]

Jesus put his servants on notice too. In Luke 12:35-37, 40, he says:

> "Be dressed ready for service and keep your lamps burning, like servants waiting for their master to return from a wedding banquet, so that when he comes and knocks they can immediately open the door for him. It will be good for those servants whose master finds them watching when he comes. . . . You also must be ready, because the Son of Man will come at an hour when you do not expect him."

The deeper the night, the nearer our master's return. Long darkness dulls and wearies us. The bewildering demands of the COVID-19 shutdown exhausted churches and their leaders. So imagine the weight on Christians being persecuted! It is not easy to manage the household while waiting in the wee hours for the master to come back for us, but Jesus promises, "It will be good for those servants whose master finds them ready, even if he comes in the middle of the night or toward daybreak" (Luke 12:38).

What does it mean for Christ's servants to "be dressed ready for service" with our "lamps burning"? It means that "faithful and wise" leaders talk often enough of Christ's return that his people do not grow slack in their yearning for him, nor begin living as though his return didn't matter (Luke 12:42). I grew up in a church and era when we were

WHEN THE UNIVERSE CRACKS

indoctrinated with end times expectations. I recall being jittery about walking on the wrong side of Main Street, the side with the movie theater and two bars, lest Jesus come back and find me so near temptation. No one thinks that way now, at least not in my circles, but it would serve us well to always have in the back of our minds: *What if Jesus came back right now?*

In this same scenario, Jesus gives us an extraordinary promise worth waiting for: "Truly I tell you, he will dress himself to serve, will have them recline at the table and will come and wait on them" (Luke 12:37). Think of that! We are ushered to the wedding feast, humble servants all of us, only to find that the master of the feast—yes, our Bridegroom, Jesus—puts on servant's clothes and brings the bread and wine to *us*! That is worth staying up all night for!

"The faithful and wise manager, whom the master puts in charge of his servants," has two duties: to keep God's people ready for his return and "to give them their food allowance at the proper time" (Luke 12:42). Meal after meal, week after week, year after year. To feed them is to prepare them, to strengthen them, to nourish their love for Christ and for one another, to help them abide in Christ. Even if a storm rages outside the door, even if we grow weary and beleaguered, God's servants must always be fed a steady diet of grace and truth in Christ Jesus. In God's good time, Jesus will not only serve us but he also promises this: "Truly I tell you, he will put him in charge of all his possessions" (Luke 12:44).

"I Know Where You Live"

Outside of the Gospels, Jesus spoke at length one other place in the New Testament—when he addressed the seven churches in Revelation 2–3. These churches were not facing a pandemic, but they were each under intense pressure. Jesus walked unseen among them and sent them notification of what he saw. Churches, of course, are not always what they seem. Only Jesus sees us as we really are. As with those seven, Jesus walks among our lampstands, speaking to the messengers of our churches, seeing if we will listen to what the Spirit says.

For example, Jesus saw that the Ephesians had "persevered and . . . endured hardships for [his] name" (Revelation 2:3), yet their first love (for one another, I think) had grown cold. He saw Smyrna's "afflictions and . . . poverty" (Revelation 2:9) and Pergamum's diabolical government ("where Satan has his throne," Revelation 2:13). He saw the wolves lurking without and within those churches, as well as the besetting sins of several congregations, but he also saw their bravery and faithfulness. Seven times in Revelation 2–3, Jesus promised a rich reward to "the one who is victorious." There it is again—the urging to persevere under pressure. "Be faithful, even to the point of death, and I will give you life as your victor's crown" (Revelation 2:10).

Churches these days have been big on self-analysis—surveys, alignment teams, consultants. They have their place, I suppose, but I always wished Jesus would just give us one of those succinct letters, even if it would be hard-hitting.

However else congregations prepare for the future, uncertain as that can be, we should humbly wait on Jesus to tell us himself how he assesses us. What pleases him? Where are we found wanting? What promise would he lay in our hands? Again, to be prepared for tomorrow, we must pray today, with fasting to sharpen our attention, lest we come unprepared to the dark hour. A Chinese proverb says, "Don't wait until you are thirsty to dig a well."

The Unprayed Prayer

On that dark, final night of his mortal life, Jesus led his disciples out to the garden of Gethsemane, where he told them, "Watch and pray so that you will not fall into temptation" (Matthew 26:41). Danger was nearer and more diabolical than they imagined. That is Jesus' warning for Christians, one and all, on the verge of great trouble that we may not see coming. Luke 21:36 puts Christ's warning this way: "Be always on the watch, and pray that you may be able to escape all that is about to happen, and that you may be able to stand before the Son of Man." His warning is all the more serious because it remains true that "the spirit is willing, but the flesh is weak."

Jesus taught us that one of our most basic prayer requests is, "Lead us not into temptation, but deliver us from evil." Yet we often forget to pray it. Apart from a recitation of the Lord's Prayer, when was the last time you heard that petition in church or found it on the list for your small group? Jesus told Simon Peter that night, "Satan has asked to sift all of you as wheat" (Luke 22:31). I'm sure Satan never stops pestering God for that permission. There is comfort knowing that Satan can only touch us with the Lord's permission, but it is sobering to remember that our prayers—humble, self-examining, urgent—are our God-given antidote to such diabolical testing. Satan succeeded in crushing Peter, not by the assault of some snarling Roman guard but by the curious comment of a servant girl, "This man was with him" (Luke 22:56). Some churches in the COVID-19 season were torn apart, not by heresy or the persecutors, but by fighting over masks! *Masks!*

We ought not only pray that terrible times will be over soon but, more importantly, that when they come, we will not sin. Many times I've told bewildered counselees, "You may not know what to do next, and God may not answer your questions, but one thing I can tell you for sure: *Don't sin.* That will certainly make things worse." And to that end, we must pray, especially in the witching hours, or we will surely fall to temptation. Likewise, our churches must pray for God to forestall the beguiling diversions and outbursts that upheavals prompt. Whether we walk through the valley of the shadow of death alone or together, we must "watch and pray," lest we fall prey to the evil one.

The Long View

Even while Christ alerted believers under pressure to the treachery of imminent temptations, he also taught us to look beyond the horizon for the cataclysmic signs preceding "the end." In Matthew 24:6-8, he said, "You will hear of wars and rumors of wars, but see to it that you are not alarmed. Such things must happen, but the end is still to come. Nation will rise against nation, and kingdom against kingdom. There will be famines and earthquakes in various places. All these are the beginning of birth pains."

These upheavals in our world are not the end times, but they're not *any* times either. They don't need to be slotted somewhere in Revelation, but they should be observed the ways sailors watch the sky or the way an obstetrician times a mother's contractions. According to Jesus, they alert us not to be deceived by those claiming to be the Messiah. They warn us that a terrible era of persecution, apostasy, and false teachers is yet to come. One thing the pandemic should have made vividly clear is that apart from God's restraint, our world can be turned upside down in a heartbeat. Riots can erupt into wars. Fires can rampage unhindered. Economies can tumble like Jericho's walls.

By the same token, Jesus made clear that when the Day of the Lord comes with Christ's return, the world around us will be unsuspecting, just as they were in the days of Noah:

> "For in the days before the flood, people were eating and drinking, marrying and giving in marriage, up to the day Noah entered the ark; and they knew nothing about what would happen until the flood came and took them all away. That is how it will be at the coming of the Son of Man. . . . Therefore keep

watch, because you do not know on what day your
Lord will come."

MATTHEW 24:38-39, 42

We cannot get our alerts from TV news bulletins, from
alarmist apocalyptic preachers or bloggers with their Bibles
only open to proof texts. Tumult is our wake-up call.

Giving God's Meaning to Calamity

In Luke 13:1-5, Jesus addressed two recent tragedies, one
a cruel, bloody act by Pilate, and another the collapse of a
tower that killed eighteen people. "Do you think that these
Galileans were worse sinners than all the other Galileans . . . ?"
Jesus asked. "I tell you, no! But unless you repent, you too
will all perish."

In a time of widespread calamity, people are much more
likely to think that God is at fault than that God is speaking. It is up to believers in such times to put things in divine
perspective. Death can strike any time, whether by cruelty
or accident, so we tell people, "Now is the time to repent.
Look how suddenly tomorrow can be snatched away!" *Repent*
is such a hard word to use these days, isn't it? Seems so . . .
what? Judgmental? But that's what Jesus told us to say. The
wise church, especially in times of catastrophe, remembers
that the gospel starts with, "*Repent* and believe the good
news!" (Mark 1:15, emphasis added).

We take our cues not only from Jesus but also from Noah.
Yet we offer a better ark than Noah's, a better shelter in the

time of storm. We welcome people to join us in the mighty fortress of God's grace in Christ. The love we have learned and practiced in our own church families can flow out into a panicky world with grace and truth. Who else will pray for them, one at a time? Who else brings Christlike capacity to bind up the brokenhearted, to feed those hungrier than they realize, to offer "a garment of praise instead of a spirit of despair" (Isaiah 61:3)?

Glenn Packiam writes, "Christians sing like it's morning even while it's midnight in the world."[3] On the last Saturday night before the coronavirus closed most of our churches, I sat with a small group of believers, all strangers to me, in a little church in western Ohio. We shared a sense of foreboding, but as Christians do, we sang, we read Scripture, and we prayed. It was my first time to sing,

When I fear my faith will fail,
Christ will hold me fast;
When the tempter would prevail,
He will hold me fast.

I could never keep my hold
through life's fearful path;
For my love is often cold;
He must hold me fast.

He will hold me fast,
He will hold me fast;

For my Saviour loves me so,
He will hold me fast.[4]

"I have told you these things," Jesus said that final night, "so that in me you may have peace. In this world you will have trouble. But take heart! I have overcome the world" (John 16:33).

7

A SPIRITUALITY OF CRISIS RESPONSE

Jo Anne Lyon

"I, Peter, am an apostle on assignment by Jesus, the Messiah, writing to exiles scattered to the four winds. Not one is missing, not one forgotten. God the Father has his eye on each of you, and has determined by the work of the Spirit to keep you obedient through the sacrifice of Jesus. May everything good from God be yours!" (1 Peter 1:1-2, MSG).

These words of Peter brought hope to the believers scattered throughout Asia Minor (modern-day Turkey). Their lives were filled with disruption, uncertainty, and persecution. Yet, throughout the letter, Peter assured them of God's presence. He did not assure them they would be spared pain, or even death. But through it all, Peter reminded them, "God's strong hand is on you" (1 Peter 5:6, MSG).

Today we are experiencing similar confusion, scattering, economic loss, health loss, death, rhythms of life turned upside down, racial tension, physical and sexual abuse, mental-health concerns, and the list goes on, such as we have never seen in recent history. Ultimately, the world is begging for a leadership that can bring peace and hope above all the clamoring voices. In this chapter, I would like to journey through some of the current places of fear and grief and ultimately get to lament. Learning to lament will result in the freedom and creativity within God's people to carry their own load as well as bear one another's burdens.

Fear

The first emotional response to crisis—even a perceived crisis—is fear. Fear is stoked by loss: The loss of what we have known. The loss of the rhythms of life. The loss of immediate relationships. The loss of control of our destiny. It feels as if our life is in the hands of an unknown person or group controlling our future. Fear increases with the number of deaths and the amount of unrest in the world.

Isolation and protectiveness become immediate effects of fear. In a state of isolation, a type of mild paranoia can set in, leading to lack of trust in others. *Where are the people like me? I cannot trust those who are different from me.* Fear also leads us to believe that the most extreme outcomes of any crisis will become reality. For example, when the stay-at-home orders for the COVID-19 pandemic were given, many families feared they would never see their loved ones again.

Many pastors also feel fear of the unknown. How do I reshape church services? How do I stay connected and pastor the people of my congregation? How do I do this in the next few days? Fear immediately exaggerates one's inadequacies and brings secondary fears of comparison and public humiliation.

I was surprised by how the church responded at the beginning of the pandemic. There seemed to be a cry by many on social media to return to the old hymns and songs that once brought peace. Frankly, I even found them comforting and found myself sitting at the piano playing hymns I had not sung or played for years. This was not bad. After all, hymns can contain great theology to remind us of the unchanging character of God. But I found the conversations then becoming divisive regarding what were accepted as songs worthy to be sung. This, again, led to isolation only with those "like me." There were limited conversations of the needs around us, and rare mention of those of other ethnicities who were experiencing loneliness and death.

In other words, isolation clothed with fear makes it impossible to reach out to others at the very time a compassionate heart would be healing to the fearful person as well as to the person in need.

When isolation is realized as one's coping method, the next impact of fear is hopelessness: "Things will never be as I have known them, and I don't know how to function in the new normal." I believe most of us experienced this feeling at times throughout the pandemic. It is a natural response.

But when one "parks" in isolation too long, hopelessness can then turn to anger.

Sadly, during the days of the pandemic crisis, I saw much of this anger turn to the church and to pastors. The reopening of churches and their changing schedules increased the number of angry emails to pastors and churches. In the same manner, the issue of wearing masks or not wearing masks escalated to the point of people changing churches, with angry outbursts to pastors and staff on their way out. These behaviors created pain and division within the church. I am concerned that we have not been teaching as Peter did: how to suffer and how to lose yet gain (1 Peter 5:10).

Yet God our Creator knew we needed to know what to do with fear. The most often repeated commandment in the Bible—"Do not fear" or "Do not be afraid"—is found hundreds of times, which says something about the God who made us and knows us.

The first time God instructed someone to not be afraid is in Genesis 15:1, in these words spoken to Abram: "Do not be afraid, Abram. I am your shield, your very great reward." It is interesting that this call to trust without fear follows three chapters of Abram's obedience. Genesis 12 articulates the call of God to Abram: a bold call, requiring total obedience. However, in verses 11-13, the ugly head of fear reared its head. As a result, Abram felt he needed to lie to save his life:

As he was about to enter Egypt, he said to his wife Sarai, "I know what a beautiful woman you are.

> When the Egyptians see you, they will say, 'This is his wife.' Then they will kill me but will let you live. Say you are my sister, so that I will be treated well for your sake and my life will be spared because of you."
>
> GENESIS 12:11-13

It appears God recognized the fear and knew that Abram could not follow the next step of God's call without God acknowledging it. God did not judge Abram for his fear; he simply named it and reminded Abram, "Do not be afraid." In the same way, we should name our fears during times of uncertainty. Doing so gives them less power and reminds us of God's presence.

Grief

As fear hangs in our culture, grief is the unrecognized sandpaper on our soul that constantly grinds at us. I hear many people say, "I feel like I want to cry deep within my body, but I really can't identify why." The rhythms of life tend to define our purpose, our relationships, our future. These have all been disrupted during the COVID-19 pandemic. Life at work has certain relationships, but now there are layoffs. Many have become unexpectedly unemployed, and businesses have closed. We worry about the children's education. Will they be able to catch up? There is particular concern about children eleven to fourteen years old, especially those in underserved areas (both rural and urban). Their education has not only been disrupted, but in many places it is nonexistent. There are projections that large numbers of students will be so far behind they will not return to school and will be vulnerable to a variety of harmful situations. The parents of these children grieve these potential losses, along with their own inability to change the situation.

What has just been described above is grief. In a sense, there has been a death of many parts of life as we have known it. The stages of grief as described by Elisabeth Kübler-Ross in her bestselling book, *On Death and Dying* (1969), are evident, including denial (*This won't last long*), anger (*This is _____'s fault*), bargaining (*What can I do to get this to stop?*), depression (*I don't want to get out of bed*), and finally acceptance (*What can I do to help someone else experiencing a similar struggle?*). I will begin to find others with whom we have shared experience. I will listen and believe we will find mutual healing. As has been well documented, these steps are not fast, and they don't work in sequence. Over the years, however, they have proven to facilitate a journey toward healing.

One example of the acceptance step mingled with the other stages is that of congregations responding to the immediate crisis of education for children in under-resourced areas. Some have repurposed their building to provide Wi-Fi, along with tutors, for children's ongoing education. I have seen grief move into comfort and hope for both the children and the congregants. This is an example of carrying one's own load and at the same time tending to the burdens of others.

Lament

The more complete healing comes only through the process of lament. Fear and grief are immediate normal responses to disruption; however, we must call people to continually move toward lament.

Lament is a spiritual discipline that calls us to reconstruct meaning when suffering leaves us disoriented. It is the ancient practice of crying out and naming our pain, disappointments, and deepest emotions, pleading for God's attention. In lament, we can weep bitterly and still sense comfort. It opens a window of light into hopelessness.

I have learned through the years that lament is a journey, both personal and corporate. It gives permission to speak one's heart and to know that God understands. These words in Lamentations are an example of this renewing process.

> I remember my affliction and my wandering,
>   the bitterness and the gall.
> I well remember them,
>   and my soul is downcast within me.
> Yet this I call to mind
>   and therefore I have hope:
>
> Because of the LORD's great love we are not consumed,
>   for his compassions never fail.
> They are new every morning;
>   great is your faithfulness.

LAMENTATIONS 3:19-23

Jesus was no stranger to lament. His words, "Come to me, all you who are weary and burdened, and I will give you rest" (Matthew 11:28) are a gracious invitation to lament. Jesus also modeled the practice of lament as he wept over Jerusalem. In Matthew 23:1-36, he declares the woes on the city's leaders for their continual rejection of God's call for repentance. Note his words of lament in verses 37-39:

> "Jerusalem, Jerusalem, you who kill the prophets and stone those sent to you, how often I have longed to gather your children together, as a hen gathers her chicks under her wings, and you were not willing. Look, your house is left to you desolate. For I tell you, you will not see me again until you say, 'Blessed is he who comes in the name of the Lord.'"

And with some of his last words, Jesus quoted Psalm 22, a psalm of lament, while dying on the cross: "My God, my God, why have you forsaken me?" (Matthew 27:46).

The Nature of Lament

Pastor and songwriter Glenn Packiam gives a foundation for lament in his article "Five Things to Know About Lament."[1] According to Packiam, there are five characteristics of lament.

1. *A form of praise.* Lament is calling to remembrance the goodness of God, "an appeal to God based on confidence in his character." Psalm 103 is filled with praise

and remembrance of the character of God, including "Praise the LORD, my soul, and forget not all his benefits" (verse 2) and "from everlasting to everlasting the LORD's love is with those who fear him" (verse 17). Psalm 145 is praise of the highest sort in all twenty-one verses. I love the rhythm of this psalm—first a call to praise (verses 1-2), followed by the foundation based on the character of God, including his power, compassion, goodness, trustworthiness, and righteousness (verses 3-21). Our praise is strengthened as we remember the character of God.

2. *Proof of our relationship with God.* Lament is recalling God's unconditional love for us. There are over seventy verses in the Bible that speak of "remembering." God wants to continually remind us of his goodness and not rely on our skewed memory. In this step it is good to just quietly begin to name aloud or in writing specifics of God's goodness in one's life.

3. *A pathway to intimacy with God.* As Packiam explains, "The God who speaks calls us into relationship." As one laments, the desire for God becomes more laser focused. One can hear the passionate voice of God to Jeremiah: "Call to me and I will answer you, and will tell you great and hidden things that you have not known" (Jeremiah 33:3, ESV). Jesus said, "Abide in me, and I in you" (John 15:4, ESV). And James reminds us, "Draw near to God, and he will draw near

117

to you" (James 4:8, ESV). Lament becomes a place of losing ourselves in God and opening our hearts for him to act.

4. *A call for God to act.* New Testament theologian N. T. Wright says, "When we are indwelt by the Holy Spirit, then somehow, God is praying within us for the pain around us." Naming our pains, struggles, fears, and weaknesses—and allowing the Holy Spirit to pray through us—is freeing. It is in this phase that our hearts are opened to the suffering around us. We can *see*.

5. *Participation in the pain of others.* This stage leads us from personal pain and isolation to the step of empathy and ultimately solidarity with the suffering, thereby becoming the community of Christ. Paul strongly states: "If one part suffers, every part suffers with it" (1 Corinthians 12:26). "Every prayer of lament which we offer is another 'Amen'" to the prayers of our brothers and sisters in Christ. Creativity, imagination, and freedom are released in God's people to be the voice, action, and hope above the clamor of noisy confusion. This is the hope people are begging to see and experience.

The Practice of Lament

The question I hear over and over is, "How can I/we lament?" I'm sad to say it, but the practice of lament has been largely absent in the contemporary White Western church. In my observation, it simply does not support the cultural triumphalism that permeates the White American evangelical church. As a result, the practice of lament has been lost. Here are some examples and practical suggestions for incorporating the practice of lament both corporately and individually.

Corporate Lament

The first time I participated in a service of lament was in Freetown, Sierra Leone, after a horrific rebel attack on the city during their civil war in 1999. I thought I was going to a memorial service—but not so. The pastor opened with a reading of Psalm 42. This is a classic psalm of lament, in which the psalmist names the troubles endured in exile as well as the sense of remoteness from God. As the pastor slowly read the psalm, members of the congregation responded with groans and spontaneous cries of "Lord, have mercy." As the moans and groans were uttered, I thought of Paul's words in Romans 8:26 and knew the Spirit was interceding: "The Spirit helps us in our weakness. We do not know what we ought to pray for, but the Spirit himself intercedes for us through wordless groans."

Following the reading of the psalm, one of the pastors stood and began to read the names of all congregation members who had lost their lives during the siege, along with their age and cause of death. Again, the congregation responded with muffled weeping, groans, and words of prayer during the reading. He concluded by referring to the last verse of Psalm 42: "Put your hope in God, for I will yet praise him, my Savior and my God." The choir then followed, singing a cappella in beautiful, hushed harmony, a song they had composed for this occasion, "We are on a journey . . . We will not give up hope." They sang slowly. The words were carefully enunciated, and phrases were repeated for emphasis. The swaying of participants to the music expressed a hopeful visual. It felt like both a dirge and a hymn of hope. I was then invited to follow with words of consolation from denominational leaders around the world. Frankly, I don't think my words meant anything; the significant part was my presence. They were reminded that their greater church community had not forgotten them. They were not alone. There is a personal, mysterious connection I have had with the people of that service this many years since.

From that service, I saw a freedom emerge with new courage to respond to the suffering in the city. Some leaders transformed their churches into hospitals for mothers and their babies, who were nearly starving without enough breast milk. Others cared for unaccompanied children and started informal schools. One pastor told me, "I felt I didn't have the energy to do this. But as I took care of others, I was taking care of myself." Another leader said, "I had so much bitterness toward the rebels, but somehow in that service, I found forgiveness in my heart toward them. I have been released." I believe that as congregations lament corporately, they are drawn together with new unity and creative direction of the Holy Spirit.

Most pastors are fearful of a public service of lament.

Generally, pastors tell me they just simply feel awkward and fearful they will say the wrong thing. But after leading one, they realize the Holy Spirit is present. Following are just a few simple guidelines.

- A public service of lament must have a specific purpose, which should be named at the beginning.
- This service should be led by the senior or lead pastor, thereby communicating its high importance to the congregation.
- Explain how the service will proceed.
- Give examples of lament in Scripture, and describe the Scriptures that will be used. Other pastors and lay people may read appropriate Scriptures. Some of the Scriptures to be used may be Psalms 5; 13; 35; 42; 137; Jeremiah; Lamentations; and Habakkuk.
- Explain how people will be expected to pray: whether with responsive reading, silent prayer, sentence prayer, short spontaneous prayer, or another means. Select several people in advance to pray.
- Make sure there is room for silence. Explain that there will be silence—and how the Spirit moves during silence.
- It is helpful to intersperse meditative music with Scripture reading and silence.
- This should not be a long service—no more than an hour.

Personal Lament

Personal lament must become a part of regular disciplines as well. Following the 2020 racial protests in my city, a pastor who is White said, "I keep reading about a service of lament, but we can't do this corporately due to COVID-19 restrictions." He went on to say, "My heart is so heavy. I have just personally been lamenting." He shared how he had made a list of the pain he was feeling as he interacted with African Americans in his congregation. The Spirit had convicted him to great repentance about how he had not listened, how he had so many wrong assumptions without asking questions, and about his lack of empathy in so many areas. He told me he simply read those aloud in prayer. The more he read, the more he had a sense of entering the pain of his fellow brothers and sisters. In addition, as he began to spontaneously weep, he experienced both comfort and a new compassion for the brothers and sisters of our city. This has resulted in his relationship with his African American brothers and sisters becoming significantly stronger: They are working together through public statements and actions. Somehow the mayor of the city saw and read these and as a result requested their presence at the "table" to assist in revising systems that tend toward racism!

In Scripture, Psalm 13 provides a moving example of personal lament:

How long, LORD? Will you forget me forever?
How long will you hide your face from me?

How long must I wrestle with my thoughts
    and day after day have sorrow in my heart?
    How long will my enemy triumph over me?

Look on me and answer, LORD my God.
    Give light to my eyes, or I will sleep in death,
and my enemy will say, "I have overcome him,"
    and my foes will rejoice when I fall.

But I trust in your unfailing love;
    my heart rejoices in your salvation.
I will sing the LORD's praise,
    for he has been good to me.

Following the example of the psalmist, here is a suggested progression for personal lament:

- Turn to God and name your pain (verses 1-2).
- Boldly ask for help (verses 3-4, corresponding with Hebrews 4:16).
- Make a choice to trust (verses 5-6).

This pattern can be used verbally in prayer, or by writing one's own psalm of lament. It is important to remember that a lament ends in hope and trust in the everlasting God. We come to him with our sorrow and listen for his loving response.

◆　　◆　　◆

This chapter has only begun the conversation regarding a spirituality of crisis response. Grappling with the results of fear and grief is not pleasant or easy work. Yet at the same time, we must understand how people can be free to find the hope they crave. I am praying your imagination has been piqued to further practice and explore the discipline of lament, both personally and corporately. As a result, may the practice of lament result in healing, restoration, and creative action in caring for oneself and others in order to embrace the vision God has for all. As Peter writes:

> Keep a firm grip on the faith. The suffering won't last forever. It won't be long before this generous God who has great plans for us in Christ—eternal and glorious plans they are!—will have you put together and on your feet for good. He gets the last word; yes, he does.
>
> I PETER 5:10, MSG

8

GROWING A CHURCH
IN THE RUINS

Kyuboem Lee

For many Christians in the US today, navigating the future—a territory rendered uncharted by multiple crises—and growing a church might feel like a daunting proposition, if not an impossible one. How do you navigate the unknown? In a crisis, it is necessary for us to prayerfully pause, redirect our focus to the basics of the church's mission, deconstruct how the old "normal" hid the larger crises that the church ignored for too long, and reimagine a design by which we might build the church anew in the ruins. A crisis has the potential to open new possibilities; the hope of rebuilding the church more faithful to the mission of God may lie on the other side.

As an analogy, consider the development of modern cities. They grew not through a smooth evolution but in fits and starts, via a series of disasters. That history shows how cities might cope with the COVID-19 pandemic—cities have faced existential crises before and have remade themselves to mitigate not only the immediate crisis but also address larger ones.[1]

For instance, in 1835, after a disastrous fire wiped out Lower Manhattan because firefighters could not access the frozen river water, New York City responded by building the Croton Aqueduct. It piped in fresh water from upstate, providing an ever-ready supply of water not only for firefighters but also clean drinking water to the city's residents. The city's leadership had been aware of the water-supply problem but did not do anything about it until a disaster forced them to act. In this way, disasters became engines that drove the dynamic transformation of cities.

Similarly, our present crisis presents an opportunity to shape the church in transformative ways. It can reveal the larger crises that we have ignored for too long and provide the urgency to finally act decisively.

True, a crisis not only presents opportunity but also danger. When Youngstown, Ohio, was struck with the crisis of the manufacturing industry departing the Rust Belt, it was abandoned instead of transformed. Youngstown, whose residents were by and large working class, did not elicit the same urgency that Lower Manhattan did. As journalist Derek Thompson explains, "Not all calamities summon forth the better angels of our nature. A complete survey of urban disasters might show something closer to the opposite: 'Status-quo bias' can prove more powerful than the need for urgent change."[2] This applies to churches, too. Insisting on as speedy a return as possible to large public Sunday gatherings during the pandemic despite obvious public health hazards is an instance of "status-quo bias" at work.

If we can find a way to overcome this bias, however, there is an opportunity for the church to re-emerge from calamity better than before.

The Crisis That Revealed a Greater Crisis

In March 2020, as the American public was only beginning to grasp the growing scope of the global pandemic, we suddenly went into a shutdown. We were instructed to stay home and work remotely. Our children could not go to school. And churches could no longer meet in person—many scrambled to find ways to broadcast their Sunday services online instead. Initially, many of us thought (wishfully, as it turned out) that the shutdown would last a few weeks and we would return to normal. But the shutdown dragged out for months—as of this writing, although many restrictions have eased here in Philadelphia where I live, we are in shutdown week thirty-two.

Pastors began wondering out loud to me if their churches would survive financially. They fretted about their buildings, sitting empty week after week. They worried about drop-off in online service attendance. They were concerned about giving amid sudden job losses and economic downturn. There is much cause for deep anxiety, and some have pushed for as quick a return to the old normal as possible.

But I don't believe that this time is one that we simply need to recover from. As the wildfires ravaging the western states—each year more deadly than the year before—portend the larger crisis of global climate change, the crisis faced by churches in the pandemic points to larger crises.

At this point, I feel it necessary to show my cards. In *The Shaping of Things to Come*,[3] Frost and Hirsch issue a call for the Western church to pivot from a Christendom mode to a missional mode appropriate for post-Christendom. The culture has undergone a massive paradigm shift; but the church in the West has largely failed to shift with it—status-quo bias at work, surely. Hence a slowly developing crisis has been overtaking the church. The pandemic, though, can present a moment of clarity to perceive our need for reinvention for the sake of mission. Many church leaders may find themselves disagreeing with my analysis, and since I lack the space here, I would encourage you to wrestle with Frost and Hirsch directly. Generally speaking, the closer you are to a postmodern cultural context, the more you will resonate. But even if you are firmly in the Bible Belt or living among neighbors with a modernistic outlook (as opposed to a postmodern one), culture change is likely on its way. It might be good to prepare now.

What are the contours of the larger crisis that this pandemic has revealed?

One, we have become overly dependent on a mode of church that invests most of our time, efforts, and resources on large-gathering productions on Sundays.

When church leaders switched over to online platforms, they faced the blank eye of the camera. There was no feedback, interaction, or engagement. Pastors found themselves seemingly preaching into the void. But isn't this the way things had been for a while? The goals of "doing church" had been polished worship experiences, marketing the church to visitors and members alike, featuring one-way monologues by preachers relying on their oratorical skills and personal charisma to get the gospel message across and build a ministry.

This attractional model of church had already been failing to connect with the younger generation of Christians,[4] as well as with the "Dones"—longtime Christians who had become disillusioned with prevailing models of church and dropped out.[5] Why? One of the Dones explained, "I'm tired of being lectured to. I'm just done with having some guy tell me what to do."[6] This speaks to the problem of clericalism and the disengagement of the laity. The pandemic only accelerated the disengagement already underway.

Two, we have become addicted to money and its representations, like buildings. Instead of resources being used for the common good and to meet the needs of the community's most vulnerable, church resources had been mostly tied up with buildings, staff, and programs.

When the pandemic hit, we found ourselves suddenly cash strapped. The financial challenge had been a growing one for the church, however. It is a common sight to see church buildings getting remade as condos. Many seminary graduates, finding traditional employment in the ministry drying up, opted for the bivocational route or no ministry position at all. When churches could not use their own buildings due to the pandemic, they became portraits of a top-heavy church budget, spending more on itself than it could afford.

Three, the church has a massive witness problem. Outside the confined world of churchgoers, it has been increasingly difficult for the church to be seen as a credible source of truth. This is not only because the culture at large has been overrun by secularism—much of the damage has been self-inflicted.

In the midst of the pandemic, the nation was gripped by racial unrest and calls for justice. The response of the evangelical church was mixed at best. As one wry observer noted, "I'm afraid evangelicals are more concerned about Critical Race Theory than they are with racism."[7] This highlights the larger history of racism in the American church.[8] As long as this denial persists, the gospel message of the new community of Christ will continue to be undermined.

Four, pastoral ministry has been in need of reform; the pandemic has further exposed this. Pastors were expected to major in personal-celebrity appeal and dynamic leadership. A consolidation of power and, too often, its abuses have been the result, as was the growing disengagement of the laity. With the arrival of the pandemic, pastors' isolation from the rest of the faith community became palpable, but it had already been there. The new center of spiritual life, worship, and discipleship became more clearly the home—but the spiritual leader could only speak into it, one way, through a screen. A discipleship that grows spiritual leaders in every household had been absent in too many churches.

These are some of the interrelated manifestations of a confluence of crises: The church lives in a post-Christendom world but has not kicked its Christendom habit of power, privilege, and wealth; the church seeks to carry out its mission via church-industrial complex philosophy and methodology—a modern, mechanistic worldview ill-suited to our postmodern world; and the church is invested in a consumerist spirituality that lacks a sense of prophetic calling and so has lost credibility and spiritual authority. These crises have been pointed out, analyzed, and talked about for years, but a sudden cataclysm may be what finally brings the church to a point of paradigm shift.

The Opportunity That Arises from Crisis

In 2011, when David Kinnaman surveyed the bleak landscape of Millennials' disengagement from church, he nevertheless struck this hopeful note:

> Tensions between faith and culture can give rise to
> new forms of cultural and social engagement, and the
> decline of the celebrity-driven Christian subculture
> creates space for local, real-life relationships with
> genuine Christ-followers.[9]

This hopefulness comes from an understanding of Christianity that is missional. The mission of God moves forward not because the church enjoys worldly power and privilege but because the Spirit of Christ safeguards and leads his church to new life—in sometimes surprising, fresh ways!—through hardships and crises. By "missional," I don't mean tacking ministries and programs that serve those outside the church onto a come-to-us, attractional ministry of Christendom. With Frost and Hirsch, I want to see churches rediscover their mission and sentness to the world, rearrange everything for the sake of reaching their post-Christendom context, and become go-to-them, incarnational churches. As Paul said, "I have become all things to all people so that by all possible means I might save some" (1 Corinthians 9:22). This applies not only to individual missionaries but to the whole people of God, with implications for the way we do church.

A Christendom understanding of mission has to do with expansion, occupation, and conquest, in line with colonialist policies of old European empires. The mission of Christendom is thus inherently triumphalistic; it naturally grasps for comfort, power, and privilege for the church. The assumption that the church has a right to the center of culture is behind the centrality of big Sunday gatherings, power-consolidating clergy, and bias for the status quo against prophetic calls for reform and justice. In contrast, in the missional stance, the mission of the church is inherently cruciform; in this paradigm, the mission finds its home, its true self, within a crisis. Growing bigger, doing more, or having a larger influence is not the point; to be in solidarity with the marginalized is, because the church, and its Lord, is marginalized in this world (Hebrews 13:12-14).

David Bosch said, "It is . . . *normal* for Christians to live in a situation of crisis."[10] It is to its detriment that the church doesn't acknowledge this reality because it became too comfortable and lost sight of its identity and mission. Bosch continues, "Let us also know that to encounter crisis is to encounter the possibility of truly being the *church*."[11] These are words for our time.

You still might not be convinced. Besides wrestling with Frost and Hirsch, and with Bosch whom I quoted, I would suggest you listen to the young people who have left church, as described by Kinnaman. Take time also to listen deeply to why non-Christians might like Jesus but not his church. The way we have been doing church—and not Christ and his gospel message—might be why.

I hope you can see why I believe that our present crisis could be an opportunity for the church to reset, pivot from Christendom, and wholly embrace the journey of becoming its true self for such a time as this. The church has been granted the theological imagination to reinvent and rebuild. For people of resurrection, death becomes a doorway out of which a new life emerges. So we do not pine for a return to normal as our deliverance, but we long for a resurrection that overshadows the old life. A crisis might not be a grave but a womb. Our resilience comes from our theology of resurrection.

The Shape of a Church Forged by Crisis

What are the new possibilities opened for the church, now that we have been afforded a crisis? I offer a few strokes of a sketch.

Pastors Will Reframe Their Roles in the Church

Instead of Sunday preaching their major work and visionary, charismatic leadership as CEO their chief metaphor, pastors will shift their focus to discipling, developing, and deploying other leaders, cultivating the gifts of the whole congregation, and convening the community to seek the leading of the Spirit for the body. There will be a pivot from consolidating power to decentralizing it.

The recent rise of the bivocational pastorate makes this pivot almost necessary. In this framework, the ministry is not the pastor's alone; the ideal is the priesthood of all believers. The missiologist Roland Allen had this in mind when he spoke of "the spontaneous expansion of the church"—what happens when the church is freed from clericalism and the laity becomes essential actors (not spectators) in the common missional life of the Spirit.[12]

Related to the shifting role of the pastor is a shift in our theology of church.

Our Theology of Church Will Shift

We are in the habit of thinking of churches as institutions housed in buildings with a class of professionals running them. But the pandemic has shown just how frail the linkage between the church as an institution and the Christian household isolated during a pandemic can be. Moving forward, the apostolic DNA latent in each household needs to be activated. This is a possibility when every believer in the church is already on the discipleship path of cultivating and exercising their leadership gifts in community. Spiritual leadership in households becomes a natural outflow.

Alan Hirsch has championed fivefold leadership gifting of the church to call the whole church, not just the clergy, back to its missional vocation and identity. It is a theology of church that has been dubbed "movement ecclesiology"[13] because church is conceived as a movement growing from the grassroots, not an institution that operates top-down. The leadership potential already resides within each gathering of disciples, no matter how small (even individual households), and when these groups are activated, multiplied, and networked, we have an organic movement that has the capacity to work and grow spontaneously, led by the Spirit.[14]

Movement ecclesiology is well suited for life in the ruins. When institutional superstructures become obsolete, church communities don't get hung up on status-quo bias, but rather reimagine, reinvent, and reforge a new way forward because we always had what we needed all along. This is how Jesus did his community—he shared all his life together with his disciples as they participated in ministry together. This becomes the archetype for "the organic people movement" that we call church, for our time.[15]

Tod Bolsinger, writing specifically for the kind of leadership that the pandemic calls for, notes that in order to prepare for the unknown, we will need strong communities that nurture a high level of trust and engage in common work and life.[16] Small groups of disciples on mission can provide strong community in ways large-group Sunday gatherings cannot.

Thus we can grow our community's ability to adapt quickly and effectively, no matter what crises may come our way, without being thrown into a panic because we suddenly find that we had relied overmuch on the comforts of our institutional structures. What is needed at this time of crisis, more than ever, is a decentralization of leadership, resources, and power and detoxing from our addiction to money, building, and clericalism.

But how are we supposed to cultivate community during a pandemic, when we have been cut off from each other?

The pandemic has opened some surprising possibilities. For instance, some formed "pandemic bubbles." They entered a covenant of sorts to share a life together for the duration of the crisis and mitigate mounting stress on individual families. This arrangement has enabled them to share childcare, schooling, cooking and other chores, as well as provide an outlet for relational needs that a nuclear family cannot on its own. These bubbles point us to important possibilities for how we conceive of church.

David Brooks wrote about the history and limitations of the American nuclear family in his article, "The Nuclear Family Was a Mistake," and showed how our society has been adapting and creating new forms of family—forged families and fictive kins. These new extended families are becoming more widespread as the nuclear family has receded. Instead of trying to hold on to the nuclear family as the ideal (which has led to increasing isolation and loneliness), it is time to welcome the new norm, Brooks exhorts. "It's time to find ways to bring back the big tables."[17]

Of course, a church is more than fictive kinship—it is spiritual kinship, a community of many made one by Christ. When the church sought to behave more like an institution than an extended family, its shortcomings were laid bare by rapid culture change and the pandemic. Might this moment signal a call to reclaim this nature of the church as a new family—a "bubble" not for the sake of convenience or survival but for the sake of an alternative community of the Kingdom?

It is interesting to examine how churches used technology during the pandemic. Some focused on producing as polished a presentation of the Sunday experience as possible. But one must question the quality and depth of long-term engagement with the church of any newcomers gained this way. As those who dropped out of church can testify, not expecting new followers to do much more than sit for service, no matter how well produced, forms us into consumers and not disciples—a pitfall of an attractional church.

But others put their focus on utilizing technology to cultivate community. Instead of broadcasting Sunday service as their main focus (without necessarily doing away with it), they instead maximized the interactive capabilities of online platforms to deepen communal connections—discussing biblical teachings, encouraging each other in obedience, providing mutual emotional and spiritual support, and engaging in communal prayer. Some even found ways to have love feasts and communions online.[18]

These are creative ways to employ modern technology to return to churches' ancient roots of community.[19] In the process, they set up a new community to arise on the other side of the pandemic. These budding faith communities will need to be encouraged to continue following this path of cultivating kinship even when we emerge from shutdowns, in person and around physical tables, ready to welcome others in need of a hospitable fellowship of God seekers.

Missional-Incarnational Opportunities Will Be Revealed

When challenged to care for the hurting in their own neighborhoods and realize an embedded (or incarnational) model of church, many Christians have responded, "There aren't any poor in my neighborhood," and resorted to a tourist model of missions. Life of service was relegated to the occasional rather than being a daily reality. This perception of needs being absent in their own backyards often stems from a lack of knowledge of their own neighborhoods, however. A crisis can provide the church with a fresh missional-incarnational opportunity.

Along with many in our society, Christians have often neglected to take seriously their place and situatedness. We were not taught to be good students of our communities; instead, we were taught to be committed to the church as an institution. The result was that we became good Christians but lousy neighbors.[20] An institution can create its own ever-increasing demand to be taken care of, instead of facilitating mission. Much energy and time is required to run the programs, fund the ministry, and build the building. So many Christians become absent from their own blocks, where young people who need mentors or families get their needs met not from God's people but from street gangs. The church must rediscover its incarnational mission and its calling to solidarity with the hurts and the joys of its parish.

But when the insatiable demands of the church-industrial complex are interrupted, we have the opportunity to look around our neighborhood and reset. Those who are struggling with hardship are now as readily apparent as food-bank lines stretching down our communities' thoroughfares or tent cities springing up in our downtown districts. As our world shrank, many of us became engaged with our immediate neighbors and their needs. We went on grocery-shopping runs for them; we displayed signs of encouragement on our windows; we formed text-messaging chains. Church buildings that were sitting empty got turned into community centers to mobilize neighbors to distribute food to the hungry and fearful, to get organized for community interests, and to simply support each other in times of need, as neighbors should.

In the wake of crisis, some churches will need to merge with others. Is it possible to imagine such a merger with an eye toward the needs of our world? I am thinking especially of racial justice. If churches are going to be reconfigured anyway, why take the easiest possible road and keep congregations homogeneous? Instead, should we not imagine heterogeneous mergers?

It is often noted, in a rueful, resigned manner, that Sunday at 11:00 a.m. is still the most segregated hour in America. What if the pandemic is giving us an opportunity to break down this segregation? Instead of simply throwing up our hands and saying, "That's just the way it's always been," shouldn't a reset of our congregations address the nation's original sin?

If so, such undertakings will need to pay careful attention to the racial power dynamics. Past efforts at multiracial congregations have been naive to White privilege and thus produced churches that imposed a melting-pot model of racial integration, papering over the hard work of racial reconciliation and justice with tokenism.[21] Going forward, we will need to take care that multicultural congregations will feature voices of color as primary voices.

Building renewed congregations and missional communities in the aftermath of a crisis will not be easy. But our society and our churches may finally be more ready than ever for such bold, embodied gospel witness. Indeed, building such faith communities is what will give credibility to our witness.

◆　　◆　　◆

These are but a few sketches of how churches could rebuild in the ruins, if they are able to overcome their status-quo bias, to reset and emerge from the pandemic as incarnational communities. Many details will vary greatly from one local context to another, from one congregation to another; there will be many unexpected surprises, some pleasant, others not as much; there will be delightful creativities and breakthroughs; there will be hardships that will require the perseverance of the saints. We will need to learn to wait and listen to the leading of the Spirit as God leads, step by step—another pivot from a self-confident Christendom mode. May the Lord lead us into the new, uncharted land with faith and expectancy. He can make everything new, including us, his church.

9

HE HAS SHOWN US WHAT IS GOOD

Catherine McNiel

I JOINED THE GYMNASTICS TEAM in junior high. Well, in a manner of speaking. My family had just moved to a new town, and for the first time, I lived somewhere offering gymnastics. I had always wanted to learn to flip and tumble and fly through the air like my favorite athletes on television, but I was already thirteen years old and couldn't even land a cartwheel. Still, this was my first and last chance, so day after day, with Whitney Houston singing in the background, my classmates tossed their bodies higher and higher into the sky while I tried to make my back bend enough to touch the floor.

It would be too generous to call me a bench warmer. A team includes players of various skill levels with different ways to contribute; not everyone is a star. But I didn't contribute to the team in *any* way. I did stuff in the same room as the gymnasts, but that was the extent. I made new friends but was never a teammate: I was a guest doing stretching exercises in the gymnasium. Being in the room wasn't enough to make me a gymnast. (Reader, I never did progress beyond cartwheels.)

We have a way of talking about church that reminds me of what I'll nostalgically call "my gymnastics days." As long as we're in the room where it happens, we consider ourselves part of the team. The superstars do the work, and that lets the rest of us off the hook. When crisis hits, we wholeheartedly agree "the church" should step up and do something. That's what the pastors are for, right? We have a committee for that.

But this is simply not the offer God extends when he invites us to join the body of Christ. Not during a crisis, and frankly, not ever. Following Jesus is not merely agreeing with what God is doing through the church but *joining* what God is doing through the church. We are a team, actively enrolling in Christ's body to work for God's Kingdom in the power of the Spirit. Jesus doesn't invite us to be the savior but to *follow* the savior. None of us can carry the whole thing on our own shoulders. That's okay; that's by design, actually. That's how teams work.

Friend, the invitation has arrived, and you are holding it in your hand. In the previous chapters, we have seen how crisis has engulfed the world and will again. We have observed how God's people have responded, what the Bible teaches, how history plays out. We have acknowledged that a crisis, by definition, is something we didn't see coming and have no experience surviving. And yet the crisis has come, and the question is here: What are *you* going to do? How will you join with the church in your community to be salt and light right where you are? What does it look like to follow Jesus in this crisis?

Rising from the Pew

Does your church have chairs or pews? The old pews I grew up sitting on really wore on the tailbone and backbone; today's chairs are so much more comfortable. But then again, comfortable is not what we're supposed to feel at church. Church is where we sit for a bit, drinking in nourishment and fellowship in order to stand back up and get to work. Maybe pews, those ergonomic nightmares, had something going for them: We didn't *want* to keep sitting.

In addition to comfy seating, a few American assumptions make it challenging for us to get up and follow, to actively join Jesus' disciples. First up are the twin American loves of consumerism and individualism. We think of church as a benefit or service to consume, not a community to invest in or a team to join. We sit down and receive. Enticed by marketing and programming, entertained by performers on a stage as we watch from auditorium seating—well, it sure looks like a consumer product. But unlike most institutions, the church does not exist primarily to meet the needs of its members.

The church exists to empower its members to come together and meet the needs of the full community. We are servants, not shoppers. All that we receive at church—teaching, sacraments, worship, community, spiritual formation—are the fuel that keeps us going and binds us together. In actively joining the mission of loving God and loving our neighbors, together in imperfect but committed community, we discover that our needs are met.

This brings us to individualism. We Westerners are committed to a radical new idea: that a person's primary identity is not found in their family, community, or group but within themselves; that a person's primary duty is not to the family, community, or group but to achieving personal fulfillment. Everything goes through the filter of "I" and "me." We think of sin as something an individual does, salvation as a gift God gives that individual, faith a relationship between God and one person, redemption happening in an individual life story.

On the one hand, there is important truth here. God does meet us as individuals, loving us, healing us, calling us. We cannot overstate this truth: *God is here*, loving *you*, empowering *you*, inviting *you*.

Then, as we respond to that love, that wooing, our individual relationship becomes a community affair. Like a good shepherd, God drives us together, toward each other, into a family, a flock. God takes a dangerous detour to save the one lost lamb, but he brings that one lamb back to the ninety-nine.

The question God puts to us is not only if we want a relationship with the Creator but with the Creator's people, as well. We may encounter God individually but become disciples by joining the community. We are free to love God—and enjoy God's love—from the privacy of our own individual hearts; we can even benefit from consuming the teaching, worship, and ministries on tap at our local church. But individual consumption does not create disciples. Disciples are active members of Team Jesus. Christianity is something we *practice*.

Here's another way to look at it. The truth—the glorious, miraculous, joyful truth—is that each of us was saved by grace. There is nothing, *nothing* we could do to earn the love and delightful relationship God offers us. Life is all gift, all grace.

And now, having been born into the family of God, we have work to do, together. My children did not earn the right to be born or a place in my home or the money to pay for the roof over their heads; yet they cannot sit around playing video games all day. If I pass out the chore lists and hear "But mom, you welcomed me into the family through grace! Your love is unconditional!" I would laugh, hug them tight, then start counting down from three. Yes, my love and their place in the family are unshakable. We belong together. And also, there is work to be done which I cannot do without them: food to cook and dishes to wash and bathrooms to clean. The tasks do not take away their place in the family; their delightful position in the family is where the duties come from in the first place!

Friend, hear me say this, once and for all: God does not

ask you to earn his love or a seat at the table. God loves you with an everlasting love—you, individual you. God delights in you with singing, shelters you like a mother eagle nurturing her eaglets, gathering them under her wings. Praise God in the highest heavens for this endless grace!

And, now that we are in the family, one of the gifts God provides is work for us to do together. *And there is so much work to do.*

Practicing Christianity During Crisis

If you (like me) spent decades thinking that Christianity was primarily something for individuals to consume or believe, we'll need to explore what it looks like to *practice* Christianity as a community, particularly during a crisis. To be honest, there's not one simple formula. What you can do will depend on your gifts, experiences, and resources, as well as the needs and opportunities surrounding you. It will be different for me. It will be different for your neighbors, different for your Facebook friends. We can't all be a hand, can't all be a foot. By the nature of a crisis, we've been thrown in without much time to collect ourselves and prepare. It's okay that the next steps are hard to figure out, that we're confused and overwhelmed, that we're treading water.

But it doesn't have to be complicated; don't get paralyzed waiting for a hero moment. God has shown us what is good— and what is good in a crisis: Do justice. Love mercy. Walk humbly with God. Go about your daily lives in a way that benefits your city, your community.

When the COVID-19 pandemic struck in 2020, nearly every human on the planet found their lives upended to some degree, the future unknowable, the present unrecognizable. Some responded by making things worse for themselves and everyone around them. Others did their best, one day at a time, to keep going, keep building into their families, keep seeking the good of their communities and cities.

Where I live, a high percentage of my neighbors work on crowded factory lines, pulling double shifts for employers who do not offer sick time, health insurance, or protective equipment. As a result, illness swept through our neighborhoods swiftly, taking down extended families who shared small apartments. Since many of these same neighbors have limited health care and English skills, they often didn't know where to turn for help. One man, in his zeal to protect his wife and young children, burned his work uniform to kill the germs he caught at the factory. Then, after weeks of unpaid sick leave, he had no money to buy a new set of clothes and therefore could not return to work. Another neighbor could not figure out how to buy food for the family when every member was too ill to enter the store. Yet another faced a choice of buying the medicine that might save their lives or pay the month's rent and avoid eviction. Some very recent arrivals to our country did not know how to connect their children to online school, or even how to call 911 when their loved ones became desperately ill.

Individuals in my community came together as a group, as we learned about each specific need. It didn't look the same for everyone. Some shopped for at-risk neighbors. Some served the greater good by staying home, cheering people through creative online videos, sidewalk-chalk messages, or songs belted out of windows at predetermined times. One man delivered food, supplies, and even library books to folks who were quarantined and unable to work or shop; many, many people banded together to collect all those needed items, enough to go around. One woman ran a virtual baby shower for an immigrant neighbor who was due to deliver a baby but did not yet have friends or family in the area to help her, was quarantined from work, and had no way to buy supplies. Day after day, diapers and clothes and baby things arrived at her door from people she did not even know. Another woman translated health and safety materials into the needed languages so that everyone, sick or healthy, knew the latest information and how best to care for themselves and their families. Several people made phone calls to see what was needed, explain where testing could be done, and what help was available. Still others helped cover rent so families could have food, medicine, *and* stay in their homes. One church took the money they saved on running a building—$2,000 a month—and redirected the entire sum to meeting the basic survival needs of people in town. Imagine how many miracles this basket of loaves and fishes made possible, in Jesus' name!

No one person carried our community through this crisis and yet, all the work was done by individuals, working together, forming a team to bring God's love and provision to the people around us, to seek the peace of our city during a time of crisis. No one had prepared for this particular crisis except through lifelong practices of compassion, listening, and getting to know their neighbors—including the sorts of neighbors we prefer to avoid thinking about. When the crisis came, and the need was overwhelming, each person did their part and we survived. It wasn't the pastor who did the heavy lifting or a committee—it was *us*.

Like the old army-recruitment poster declares, the church needs *you*. Not to be a consumer or a lone ranger and certainly not a savior; just an active member, doing whatever it is you do best and doing it for the Kingdom of God, a Kingdom becoming visible and tangible right here inside your own community.

Let's Get Going

Now, enough talking! Let's get started. As the prophet Micah said, "God has shown you what is good and what the Lord requires of you" (Micah 6:8, paraphrased). Let's imagine what it might look like to join God's team and practice following him during this crisis.

Walk Humbly with God

This is where it all begins; we can't do anything on our own strength. The world is engulfed in crisis, and so are you. This catastrophe may not allow space for long quiet times with the Lord, but we still need to keep our eyes on God.

- *Breathe.* Take a deep breath—inhale slowly, hold for a moment, then exhale. This breath, this moment of life, is a gift from God and your closest tool at hand to refocus your mind and body on God's presence. However chaotic this disaster may be, whatever self-care and spiritual practices must be put on hold for a season, you breathe each day, each minute. Find God here. Receive God's peace and shelter.

- *Prayer of Examen.* This simple discipline was developed by Saint Ignatius of Loyola for his community to remain mindful of God's presence during busy days. First, remind yourself of God's presence. Second, look around yourself with gratitude, and give thanks for the gift of this day. Third, consider the feelings and thoughts being stirred, inviting God to join you in them. Fourth, reflect on where there is pain and brokenness; ask for forgiveness or the strength to forgive. Finally, look forward to the coming moments or days, asking God to remain with you (spoiler: He will!) and to remind you of his presence.[1]

- *Lament.* God does not suffer from insecurity; he is more than capable of handling our grief, questions, doubts, and tantrums. Don't hide the pain of this season from God, or from yourself. Only in acknowledging real pain will you begin the process of taking control of it; silence or denial merely allows your pain to control you instead of the other way around. Join the psalmist, the prophets, and grieving people through the ages and let God hear your worst. He can take it.[2]

- *Worship.* God inhabits the praises of his people! During dark days and long, dark tunnels we can sing our way back into the light. Sometimes a few hours of worship will do it; sometimes it takes months of calling out our praises (and laments) to God. But he meets us in the process of lifting ourselves into his hands and bowing before his throne.

Love Mercy

When the chips are down, we discover what we truly love. Ourselves? Security? Money? Independence? We may be surprised to see what we're faced with at the end of the rope. We must practice loving mercy.

- *Listen.* Where are the needs in your community? Don't act in ignorance; take the time to find out what is needed, and where, and by whom. Allow this season to open your eyes to the people around you, their stories, and their voices. Don't speak over them or act for them, but *listen.*

- *Practice loving-kindness.* Prayer opens our hearts toward compassion and God's loving-kindness. As you pray, voice your anxieties and laments to God but don't stop there. Picture your neighbors, even those you don't know personally. Lift them up to God and intentionally cultivate compassion and empathy as you do. As we call forth compassion and pair it with faces and names, we will be changed on a spiritual and neurological level. We will extend mercy more effectively in person if we have learned to practice compassion in the quiet moments before God.

- *Join in.* What ministries of mercy are happening in your community? Find out. Learn what support they need. Visit (or call) churches, social-services organizations, food pantries, hospitals, and nursing homes to find out what work is already underway and how your unique resources can be useful. Once you've practiced joining in, you'll have a better sense how to act helpfully on your own.

Do Justice

In the prophet Micah's language and culture, *doing justice* meant structuring society so that all people had equal access to basic provisions. Nothing brings to light the cracks and weaknesses in our social fabric like a crisis, as people begin falling through those cracks. Once our hearts are opened through practicing mercy, our eyes begin to see injustice—that's when we join the work of reshaping society so that *all* can flourish.

- *Be a neighbor.* We make sure our loved ones are cared for, don't we? Does your tribe of loved ones include immigrants, refugees, and under-resourced people? What about people who are different from you in terms of race, ethnicity, religion, or economic status? If not, how can you make your circles more inclusive? Giving to organizations like World Relief or local outreach ministries is deeply beneficial, but nothing can beat the tender care we give to the people we love. Ensure that your tribe includes people who aren't like yourself—and then, take care of each other.

- *Start with the basics.* Who needs food right now? What about clean water, weather-appropriate clothing, secure shelter, access to employment (including a ride there and back)? What about health care and access to information—who to call, how to apply for benefits, or where to drive (and someone to translate when they get there)? You might be surprised how far beyond inconvenienced some in your community have fallen during this crisis.

- *Dig deep.* Once you're keenly, personally aware of the ways people in your community struggle against unjust and unequal social patterns, you can begin to unearth the deeply rooted systems at their foundation. Find and support the local, national, or global organizations that are raising awareness, advocating, and working toward change. Lift up voices specifically that speak from personal experience.

Follow Me

Down by the Sea of Galilee, Jesus approached Peter in the boat and said, "Follow me!" Not "Agree with me" or "Feel affection for me in your heart." Not even "Believe that what I've said is literally true." Jesus said, "Leave what you're doing behind and join what I'm doing." Peter wouldn't have done so if he didn't agree with Jesus, believe what he said, and feel affection for him. But he demonstrated all those things by getting up from the boat and walking.

Jesus came up to you in your classroom, or the nurses' station, or the board room, or your construction site and said, "Follow me." Being a disciple of Jesus means counting the cost (realizing it isn't going to be easy, there will be more trouble than you want to deal with), taking up your cross (understanding that the power holders in this world would prefer to keep the status quo, and will make you suffer if you do otherwise), and following Jesus down a narrow road (whatever they may say or believe, very few people actually *follow* Jesus). Of course, we won't follow Jesus perfectly, or even particularly well. Peter certainly didn't. Peter sank into the water! Jesus responded to one of Peter's worst blunders by saying, "Get behind me, Satan!" Peter misunderstood and misbehaved time and again, leaving Jesus in the lurch at his darkest hour. He made all sorts of errors—and yet, he remained a beloved disciple. Even after all that imperfection, Jesus built his church on Peter, the same church we joined when we decided to follow Jesus.

Most of Jesus' followers? We know nothing about them.

They aren't superstars. Just ordinary people being disciples in their churches, in their communities, changing the world one imperfect, microscopic choice at a time. But each of the hundreds of men and women who followed Jesus in obscurity had a role, contributing their own abilities to benefit the group.

Mr. Rogers, the beloved neighbor to generations of preschoolers, had advice for children during a crisis: Look for the helpers. This oft-quoted phrase was meant to encourage the smallest children to see not only chaos and pain but grown-ups working side by side to make things better. Friend, *we are those grown-ups*. While the world is in crisis, we are invited to stand with the unfailing love of God, the comfort of the Holy Spirit, and the community of brothers and sisters—and be the helpers. Our God, Creator, Sustainer, and Redeemer, is making all things new. *All things*. The broken things, the hurting things, the diseased and disoriented, the overwhelmed and marginalized. All things, new.

And—can you believe it?—God invites us to join him in the task.

10

GOD REMAINS GOOD

Matt Mikalatos

WHAT YOU'RE FEELING IS NORMAL.

The exhaustion. The questions. The anger, the fear, the uncertainty.

That's what Elijah felt when he threw himself down in the desert and said, "I'm no better than my ancestors, you should just kill me."

That's what Mary and Martha felt when their brother died . . . a death that Jesus could have stopped but didn't.

I've felt it, too, many times.

It's normal. It's human.

A few years ago, I volunteered in an immigrant community to help rebuild their houses. A hurricane had picked up their homes and taken them away. While rebuilding, we dis-covered that one of the contractors was "helping" with our crew to gain access to female volunteers he was attempting to exploit sexually. What's worse, when our leaders removed him, lawyers from our organization sent an apology for "how he had been treated."

How did I feel?

Angry. Exhausted. A hurricane is one thing, but sexual abuse on top of it? And lawyers for a Christian organization taking the side of a predator instead of their people . . . I was disgusted. How could God allow this? I thought God was good.

When I was fifteen, I lived in California, and an earth-quake collapsed a full mile of Interstate 880 in Oakland, leaving forty-two dead. The marina was on fire. Sixty-three deaths total, nearly four thousand injured, and all of this in less than a minute. A Christian pastor—not a local one—preached about the resulting devastation, and he said the earthquake was God's judgment.

I was young, but I remember wondering, *Why would God allow this earthquake, and why would God let that pastor say those things?* Is this what a loving God looks like?

As I write these words, the west coast of the United States is on fire. Over five hundred thousand people are displaced in Oregon alone, and there has been smoke thicker than fog every day for a week. We're using furnace filters strapped to box fans to help us breathe inside our homes. There are people dead and more missing. We're praying for rain . . .

begging for it. A light sprinkle could mean the difference between life and death, but so far, there's not a drop.

God, where are you? Is a little rain outside of your power?

Of course I know—we know—the answers to these questions. God is good. God is loving. God is near, God is powerful, and God knows what is happening. We affirm all this in our minds. We have it written down in our theology books. We have notes about it in the margins of our Bibles.

But maybe it's not written on our hearts.

So what I am feeling and what I believe are in conflict. There's friction between them. And so often in these moments, our temptation is to ignore those questions, those emotions, or—at the most—to review and renew our theological convictions. We remind ourselves (and others going through the same thing) that God is good/loving/God/etc. We answer the questions without addressing them. We ignore the emotions other than to say, "Those need to be brought in line with proper theology."

That is not the biblical model.

We cannot ignore the toll that crisis and trauma take on people's spirits. We cannot ignore the toll that crisis and trauma take on our own spirits.

Burned-Out and on the Run

What you're feeling, Elijah felt too.

He'd been hiding in a cave, living on water from a brook and bread delivered by birds. When the brook dried up, God directed him to move in with a widow and her son.

God gave them just enough oil and flour to feed themselves each day.

Elijah must have heard in those days about his fellow prophets being hunted and killed. No doubt he felt like we feel when the widow's son died and she shouted, "What do you have against me? Why have you come to kill my son?" Elijah prayed and God brought the boy back to life, but what kind of God would let the boy die in the first place? Maybe Elijah didn't ask that question. After all, he already knew the answer.

After three years, God sent Elijah to tell King Ahab there would be rain. Elijah gathered the people and he gathered all the prophets of the false god Baal, and he told them it was time to choose. He was the only prophet of God left. There were 450 prophets of Baal. *Figure out who is truly God and follow.*

Elijah suggested a test. Let the God who answers with fire be the true God. They put out two sacrifices. Elijah invited the prophets of Baal to pray. Which they did. For hours. They danced and shouted and cut themselves and Baal didn't answer. Elijah mocked them. "Maybe he's in the bathroom. Maybe he's on a long trip."

When Baal's prayer meeting lost everyone's interest, Elijah called them back to God's altar. He told them to douse it with water, to really soak it. When they had gotten it good and wet, he told them to do it twice more, until there was a moat around the sacrifice. The people must have looked at that precious water longingly . . . it had been three years since they had last seen rain.

Then he prayed. Nothing fancy. And God sent fire from heaven that licked up the sacrifice, evaporated the water, and sent every Israelite to their knees. They killed the prophets of Baal in the valley that afternoon, and Elijah climbed Carmel again to pray for rain.

That didn't happen right away, even though God told him that was the plan. Seven times he prayed before the black clouds came and Elijah ran home, triumphant, in the rain . . . faster even than the king's chariot.

The crisis had passed at long last.

Except shortly after that, a messenger arrived from Jezebel with a death threat, and Elijah felt what you're feeling. He was afraid. He ran.

He ditched his servant and was a full day's journey into the desert when he threw himself onto the ground and prayed to die. Why?

Because he felt like you and I feel.

He knew God was powerful . . . he had seen the fire fall from heaven. He had seen a boy raised from the dead. He had been fed by ravens.

He knew God was good. Who had saved his life so far? Who had been the one to take care of him every day the last three years?

But his heart, his emotional world, told him something else. He was afraid.

Why?

Maybe because God hadn't stopped Jezebel from killing all the other prophets in the last three years. It was the same powerful, good God who had saved Elijah that allowed the other prophets to be gutted with swords. Maybe God was good three years ago and not today.

"I've had enough, Lord," he said. Elijah felt what you feel. What you're feeling is normal.

But like you and like me, he felt guilty that his emotions and his theology were in conflict. His thoughts turned toward self-condemnation. If he had these questions, if he was so full of fear when he knew God was strong and good and loving, then he was no better than those screwed-up followers of God who had come before him. It would be better if he died. He prayed God would kill him before Jezebel found him. Exhausted, he fell asleep, completely done.

God's Response to Our Trauma after a Crisis

If you were writing the next part of the story, how would it go?

I'd be tempted to have God rebuke Elijah. "I performed a massive miracle, and you're hiding in the desert because of a death threat?"

A punishment wouldn't be out of the question.

It wouldn't be unheard-of for God to answer Elijah's prayer. "Maybe it would be best to take your life."

God wrote a different story.

Elijah wasn't ready for God's presence. He wasn't ready for a conversation. He had fears and questions and complaints, but it wasn't time to deal with those, not yet. Instead, God sent a messenger, an angel. The angel woke Elijah up and fed him—just like God had been feeding him for the last three years—and then let him go back to sleep.

Then the angel woke him again, and fed him again. "Get up and eat," he said. "The journey is too much for you."

What journey?

The journey from Elijah to God.

Elijah couldn't get into God's presence until he gathered his strength. He needed some simple, pragmatic, human things. Food. Water. Rest.

If God is good, then maybe he cares more about your health than he does about you reviewing your theology. He understands what you're feeling. He knows how the human body reacts to stress and crisis. He knows what you need.

Because God is not just good, he's patient. He's not just loving, he's slow to anger. When we are impatient with ourselves, when we are quick to anger with our own failings, we are not exhibiting godliness. Jesus said God is a good father, and what good father would give his kid a rock when he's hungry? What good father gives a kid a poisonous snake instead of a meal?

So if you think—if I think—that God's response to "I've had enough" or "I'm afraid" will be anger or judgment or punishment or frustration, we're wrong. And we will struggle to come into the presence of God if we don't eat, and rest, and take care of our bodies in the aftermath of crises.

What you're feeling is normal. Elijah felt it too.

But he slept. He ate. He drank. And, "Strengthened by that food, he traveled forty days and forty nights until he reached Horeb, the mountain of God." It was there "the word of the LORD came to him" and God reinforced and corrected his theology (1 Kings 19:8-9).

First his physical needs were met, then his spiritual ones.

Where Were You?

What you're feeling, Mary and Martha felt that too.

Their brother had died over the course of days.[1] Jesus loved them, loved their brother. They had no doubt of it. They had seen him heal the blind. They knew he had power.

They sent word via messenger, but the messenger returned alone. The loving, powerful Jesus wasn't going to intervene. So their brother breathed his last, and they wrapped him up and stuck him in a tomb. Jesus didn't even bother to come to the funeral. So the two sisters descended into grief, and questions, and weeping.

When Jesus finally arrives, Martha says, "If you had been here, my brother wouldn't have died."

In other words: Where were you?

And she follows up with a statement of belief: "Even now I know God will give you whatever you ask."

Jesus offers her some hope: "Your brother will rise again."

Martha recognizes the theological truth about a future resurrection ("I know he will rise again in the resurrection on the last day"), but that's not what she's looking for. She's asking about resurrection in the here and now.

And Jesus assures her that the resurrection is not an event. The resurrection is a person. It is Jesus himself. Jesus asks her if she believes him, and she assures him that she does.

When Mary comes, she knows how Martha feels. She feels that way, too, and she asks Jesus the same thing: *Where were you? If you had been here, my brother would not have died.*

He doesn't deny it.

Mary weeps, her friends and family weep. Jesus is deeply moved, and troubled. He weeps alongside them.

He doesn't correct them. Doesn't angrily point out that they should trust him a little more. He weeps with those who weep. He mourns with those who mourn. Even though, in his own infinite mind, he knows Lazarus will be standing beside them in moments. Even though, from God's point of view, death is a temporary state.

What Mary and Martha were feeling, I felt that too. Our family friend went through four years of cancer treatment. Four years of doctors, weeping, medication, and surgeries, and the whole time, our friend was getting weaker. When we prayed together, she often said—we often said—*where are you? We know you are good. We know you love us. We know you have the power to intervene.*

But God didn't show up, not then, and not four days later. Our friend died, and we're left with "she will rise again." The biggest questions, the hardest moments . . . many of those came after the crisis had passed.

It's natural, during times of loss, to ask if God is good. If God is good, if God is powerful, how could the Lord fail to intervene? It's the cry of Mary and Martha at the loss of their brother: *Where were you?*

When we ask those questions, God doesn't chastise us for asking the question. He might remind us of our hope ("your brother will rise again"). But in the end, he will show us not where he was, but where he has been all along. Beside us. With us. Not distant, not angry, not watching in some detached way because of his glory or sovereignty or omniscience.

We weep, and he weeps with us.

Because what we are feeling is normal. Even God feels some of those things, as it turns out.

The Compassion of the Christ

In moments of crisis—global, local, or personal—we followers of Jesus are often the first to wade in. We minister to our friends, our loved ones, our neighbors and set aside our own needs. We come out on the other side exhausted, wounded, and saying, "I've had enough, Lord." We minister in the midst of traumas even when we are also victims. Burned-out and on the run.

In the story of Elijah, we see that God encourages him to stop and take care of himself. To gather his strength for the journey to God. Empowered by his rest and the food, he travels for forty days to the mountain of God, and it's there that he hears, at last, God's voice. "Why are you here?"

Elijah tells him: They killed the other prophets, and now they're after him, too . . . the last faithful follower of God.

So God tells him to go out on the mountain because God is about to pass by. There's a mighty wind, strong enough to break rocks. Then an earthquake, then a fire. And, at last, a gentle whisper.

A still, small voice, that asks him the same question. That invites him, once again, to lay out the details of his fears. So Elijah does. *They killed the other prophets, and now they're after him, too . . . the last faithful follower of God.*

God tells him things are changing: new kings, and it's time to train a new prophet. He tells Elijah that he's not alone. In fact, there are seven thousand faithful believers "back the way [he] came" (1 Kings 19:15).

Elijah rests, gathers his strength, honestly tells God his fears, *and then* is given his marching orders from God.

In Mary and Martha's story, Jesus doesn't lecture or chastise them; he weeps with them. He mourns with them. He reminds them of the promises of God. In both stories, God *encourages those in crisis to be honest with their feelings*, to share what they are thinking. To dwell, at least for a time, in this broken place of fear and questions.

Let's not rush past that. Let's spend some time and "[sit] down in the ashes to wait for the Lord."[2] What is this crisis doing to me? To my assumptions about God, about my neighbors? How have I been broken by this crisis? Where do I need healing? What are my questions, my fears? What are my physical needs that have gone unmet?

It's not just Mary and Martha and Elijah and you and me who have felt this. What you're feeling, Jesus felt that too.

When his cousin died—his childhood friend, one of the first to believe in him, one of the few people to understand him—Jesus would have experienced the same sort of crisis we would. Unending waves of grief. Lethargy. Weeping. Pain.

Jesus is God, but he is also human. And what you are feeling, friend, as you come out of this crisis . . . that's normal. That's human.

Jesus, like Elijah, like Mary and Martha, took time to process his grief. He gathered his friends and left ministry behind for a time. They got in the boat and headed for the other side of the lake.

When they landed, the people Jesus had been ministering to have run around the lake to meet him. The quiet retreat has been replaced with the noise and clamor of people wanting something—needing something—from him. Jesus, in the midst of his own personal crisis, recognized that many of them were in crisis too. And the Scripture tells us that "he *had compassion on them* and healed their sick" (Matthew 14:14, emphasis added).

The motivating force to care for others in this time of personal crisis was his compassion. When we are in the midst of trauma ourselves, we would be wise to follow Jesus' example, and wait to minister until we are able to do it out of compassion, not obligation, not guilt, not pressing need.

How God's People Go Forth after Catastrophe

What you are feeling is normal, and the crowds are feeling it too.

Jesus saw them, harassed and helpless, like unprotected and directionless sheep.

We are tempted sometimes in crisis to focus on that coming Kingdom—and it is coming—without acknowledging the terrors and brokenness of the one we inhabit now. When our friend was going through cancer treatment, there were weeks I dropped my daughters off at Sunday school and sat alone in the parking lot. Not because I wondered if God was good. Not because I worried that God was unloving. Not because I thought God was not powerful enough to intervene . . . I knew he could.

No, I was alone in the parking lot because I couldn't bear to sit in a church that only ever talked about the ultimate triumph of Christ. They never talked about the struggle. Never mentioned any hardship. They would even skip verses in hymns that seemed too negative. They skipped over the valley of the shadow of death and went straight to "my cup overflows," and I couldn't stand it. I would weep through the worship and grind my teeth during the sermon. And that's me, not a lost sheep but a wounded one.

If we're following Jesus, if we're seeking to become like him, at some point after a crisis our attention is going to turn to the crowds. We're going to want to feed the sheep, to take care of them. We're going to be compelled to share the good news about the Kingdom. All of that is good . . . not just good, but godly. But how do we do these things in a way that is both winsome and wise? Compassion, yes, but what are some best practices to help us show authentic Christian faith in the aftermath of crisis?

Here are five ways I've seen brothers and sisters come alongside me or others in the aftermath of the worst crises:

1. *Go out to the parking lots.* I was never going to walk into that church again; I don't care how wonderful the music or how famous the preacher. Over and over, Jesus tells stories where the invitation to the Kingdom was delivered by people going out to the "highways and byways." Go to those in pain; don't wait for them to come to you.

2. *Be honest.* The first people I was able to worship with coming out of the parking lot were an African American band called Run 51. They sang songs that embraced the reality of real, systemic, ingrained, and centuries-long injustice and *then* poured out rejoicing for what God had done, was doing, and promised to do in the future. Let's not hide our pain to give the impression of the "perfect life with Christ." We're the same as those others in crisis, except we have Jesus. Why pretend all is well? In crisis, we need to share pain before sharing praise.

3. *Be prepared for the questions.* My experience is that the grieving people in the world turn their questions about God toward me and the Christian community. (*Are you good? Are you loving? Where were you?*) I need to take those questions without offense and without defending

myself or the church. They are saying that they see God in us. This is a blessing. Let's embrace them in the same way the Lord embraces us.

4. *Be present and be consistent.* "Do not fear, for God is with you." How often does God say that to us? Making sure people know we're here for the long haul—not just until their house is rebuilt, or the illness has passed, but as long as it takes—builds trust between us. We're part of their lives, not just dropping in to do charity work. When there is crisis—especially large-scale crisis—the unfolding of it may take years. Let's be committed to the long haul.

5. *Community crises require community repair.* There are griefs too heavy for one person to carry. We require a community. Everyone takes a piece of the load, and together we feel lighter. That's the defining feature of the church in Acts: "All the believers were together and had everything in common" (Acts 2:44). If we want more people to come to Jesus, sometimes the first step is to let them be together with us . . . not in a church service, necessarily, but in the intimacy and care of our community.

Sometimes our role as messengers of God may be as simple as that of the angel in the story of Elijah. Our best contribution may be to say, "The journey is too great for you" and provide a meal, encourage them to sleep.

Better Things to Come

There's a better world coming. We pray for it whenever we pray in the way Jesus taught us. "Your Kingdom come, your will be done, on earth as it is in heaven."

Where there is sickness, there will be health.

Where there is grief, there will be joy.

Where there is violence, there will be justice . . . flowing like mighty waters.

Where there is death, there will be life.

Where there is a desert, there will be streams of living water.

And God will wipe every tear from our eyes, comforting us for the losses in this life. From that time forward, there will be no more tears or crying or pain.

Remember, the voice of God was not in the hurricane, not in the wind that crushed the stones.

God was not in the earthquake.

It was not God in the raging fire.

It was *after* the storm that God's voice was heard. A still, small voice.

What you are feeling, friend, is normal.

Get up and eat. Rest. The journey from here to God may be long. Take care of your body. Prepare yourself. Better days are coming. Bring your honest complaints to God. Accept the theological promises for the future, but don't pretend they are sufficient to cover the grief of the moment. Weep and know that God weeps with you. And know that—even when we are still asking questions—we will see the glory of God in time.

God is good and God is with us.

But what you are feeling today is normal. Embrace it and let the Lord embrace you.

CONTINUING THE CONVERSATION

Questions for Reflection and Discussion

A KINGDOM CONVERSATION, such as the one this book is intended to start, has the potential, in small and big ways, to transform the world. As we allow God to bring his higher thoughts to bear on our limited vision and finite wisdom, we don't just interact thoughtfully; we do so prayerfully, subjecting ourselves to the sovereignty of a God who loves us and wants good for us and from us.

As such, Kingdom conversations take place both individually and collectively. We don't settle merely for personal reflection that deepens our private piety, or for dialogue that ends in chin-stroking self-congratulation. Rather, we engage in honest and humble conversation with God, with ourselves, and with others so that we can see where Jesus is leading us now to proclaim and demonstrate, near and far, that God is here, God is good, and God is for us.

What follows are questions to prime the pump for these Kingdom conversations. Almost every question is designed to be considered personally, for the purposes of private and public reflection and confession, and corporately, in order to listen to and learn from other perspectives, to learn to love one another, and to seek God together as a faith community.

The questions are organized by chapter in case you wish to move slowly through the book together. If you wish to discuss the book as a whole in one conversation, it's best to review the questions ahead of time and focus together on the questions that help you move from curiosity to conviction, from head to heart to hands.

Introduction

- Why did you decide to read this book?

Chapter 1: What Is a Crisis?

- In what ways have you experienced personal/internal upheaval during a recent crisis? What about in your external world, including work, church, neighborhood, relationships, and activities?
- What did this crisis reveal about your assumptions, your emotions, your relationships, your habits, your spiritual life?
- Where and how did you experience or create communitas in the midst of this crisis? What effect did this have on you?
- Would you describe yourself as energized more by hatred or by joy? What needs to change so that your focus shifts to "the joy set before us"?

Chapter 2: Notes on a Recent Crisis

- Which perspective—panoramic, peripheral, pastoral, or personal—tends to dominate your view, and which is most challenging to you?
- Have you ever felt these perspectives in tension with each other in your own life? When and how?
- How do you feel—and then how do you respond—when other people have a differing perspective about a crisis?
- Did you experience any alignment among these perspectives? How did each support the others?

Chapter 3: Crisis While the World Marches On

- How do you feel about the exposures described in this chapter?
- Do you ever feel the tension of "double consciousness" in your own life with issues regarding race?
- What have you learned from the Black Church? What else might you need to learn?
- What part is God calling you to play—individually, in your friendships, in your church, and in your community—in working for justice and racial reconciliation?

Chapter 4: A Brief History of Crisis

- Imagine yourself living during one of the historical crises described in this chapter or from your own knowledge of history. Imagine the fears and hopes,

the uncertainty, perhaps the difficult choices facing
Christians during that time. How does this inform
your perspective of the crises in our own time?

- Someday, historians will write about the crises of
2020—wildfires, racial protests, the COVID-19
pandemic, the US presidential election—as a defining
moment for God's people. What do you think
the history books will say about how Christians
responded? What do you think Jesus would say?

- What might it look like to practically live out faith
during a crisis?

Chapter 5: The Bible's Catalog of Crisis

- What gives you your identity? How were these qualities
affected by a recent crisis?

- What losses, big and small, have caused you to weep?
Why?

- What can you do to genuinely seek the welfare of
your perceived enemies when you feel like an exile or
an outsider?

- What does faithfulness look like for you in this
season?

Chapter 6: Jesus Wouldn't Waste a Crisis

- Is it easy or natural for you to view current events
through the lens of eternity? If not, what tends to
cloud your perspective?

- What is your practice regarding corporate prayer?
  When was the last time you gathered to pray with a
  group of believers? Were those prayers characterized
  by boldness and hope, or by fear? Why, do you think?
- Would you live differently if you knew Christ was
  coming back within the next month? How?
- Can you honestly say that Jesus is all you need, that
  you would be content if he were all you had? What
  gets in the way of your contentment? Be specific.

Chapter 7: A Spirituality of Crisis Response

- Which fears tend to manifest themselves most
  strongly in your life? What is your usual response to
  those fears? Do you isolate, self-protect, become angry
  or hopeless, or some other response?
- What is your experience with lament, both individually
  and corporately?
- How did your understanding of lament change or
  expand after reading this chapter?
- In what areas in your life are you holding on to
  unrealized and unexpressed grief? What will you do
  to move through lament and toward healing in those
  areas?

Chapter 8: Growing a Church in the Ruins

- What strengths and weaknesses did the COVID-19
  pandemic reveal about your church?

- What opportunities do you see for your church in the coming months?
- What must be rebuilt or reset in response to these revelations and opportunities?
- What paradigm shifts will this require? What will need to be left behind? Who will need to lead these efforts? What will be your role in this work?

Chapter 9: He Has Shown Us What Is Good

- Do you tend to think of Christianity in terms of "I" or "we"? Why?
- In what ways have you seen God's people come together in response to crisis?
- How is God inviting you to join his work in the world? What will be your next steps in response to this invitation and the needs around you? Be specific.
- Who do you see as teammates in the work of the Kingdom?

Chapter 10: God Remains Good

- What are you honestly feeling right now?
- With which biblical character and his/her struggles—referenced in this chapter or elsewhere in Scripture—do you most identify? How was God there for that person? Do you believe God cares for you in the same way? Why or why not?
- How is God inviting you to join his work in the world? What will be your next steps in response

to this invitation and the needs around you? Be
specific.

- Where have you experienced God's goodness in your
  life in the last week?
- Spend a few minutes silently in God's presence. Pray
  whatever response comes to your heart.

NOTES

CHAPTER 1: WHAT IS A CRISIS?

1. Manoush Zomorodi, "Our Relationship With Water," TED Radio Hour, NPR, August 7, 2020, npr.org/programs/ted-radio-hour/899822853/our-relationship-with-water?showDate=2020-08-07.
2. Zomorodi, "Our Relationship With Water."
3. Lee Ann Hoff, Bonnie Joyce Hallisey, and Miracle Hoff, *People in Crisis: Clinical and Diversity Perspectives*, 6th ed. (New York: Routledge, 2015), 4.
4. Durkheim introduced this term in his first book, *The Division of Labor in Society*, in 1893.
5. Émile Durkheim, "Anomic Suicide" (excerpt from *Suicide: A Story in Sociology*), in *Social Theory: Roots and Branches*, 5th ed., ed. Peter Kivisto, (Oxford: Oxford University Press, 2013), 51.
6. Brian Howard, "A Philly Trashman on Picking Up Your Garbage in the Middle of a Pandemic," *Philadelphia Magazine* (blog), August 3, 2020, phillymag.com/news/2020/08/03/philly-trashman-sanitation-workers-ppe/.
7. Tim Mackie and Jon Collins, "Apocalypse Please," April 27, 2020, *BibleProject Podcast*, produced by Dan Gummel, bibleproject.com/podcast/apocalypse-please/.
8. Dan P. McAdams, *The Redemptive Self: Stories Americans Live By* (New York: Oxford University Press, 2005).
9. Hannah Ting, "The Racialization of Face Masks," Asian American Christian Collaborative, May 28, 2020, asianamericanchristiancollaborative.com/article/the-racialization-of-face-masks.
10. As quoted in Ting, "Racialization of Face Masks," emphasis added by Ting.

11. Timothy Larsen, *The Slain God: Anthropologists and the Christian Faith* (Oxford: Oxford University Press, 2016), 193.

12. Edith Turner, *Communitas: The Anthropology of Collective Joy*, Contemporary Anthropology of Religion (New York: Palgrave Macmillan, 2012); Victor Turner, "Liminality and Community (excerpt from *The Ritual Process*)," in *Culture and Society: Contemporary Debates* (Cambridge: Cambridge University Press, 1990), 147–54.

13. Christine Jeske, *The Laziness Myth: Narratives of Work and the Good Life in South Africa* (Ithaca: Cornell University Press, 2020).

14. Hirokazu Miyazaki, *The Method of Hope: Anthropology, Philosophy, and Fijian Knowledge* (Stanford, CA: Stanford University Press, 2006), 106.

15. Zomorodi, "Our Relationship With Water."

CHAPTER 2: NOTES ON A RECENT CRISIS

1. "Listings of WHO's Response to COVID-19," World Health Organization, June 29, 2020, who.int/news/item/29-06-2020 -covidtimeline.

2. "US Leads World in Coronavirus Cases, Deaths," *VOA News*, July 7, 2020, voanews.com/covid-19-pandemic/us-leads-world-coronavirus -cases-deaths.

3. "COVID-19 Dashboard," *CSSE* at Johns Hopkins University, gisanddata.maps.arcgis.com/apps/opsdashboard/index.html #/bda7594740fd40299423467b48e9ecf6; and Adriana Diaz, "COVID-19 Was the Leading Cause of Death in the U.S. This Week, Report Says," CBS News, December 5, 2020, cbsnews.com/news /covid-19-leading-cause-of-death-united-states-this-week/.

4. World Health Organization, *Novel Coronavirus (2019-nCoV): Situation Report—22*, February 11, 2020, who.int/docs/default-source /coronaviruse/situation-reports/20200211-sitrep-22-ncov.pdf?sfvrsn =fb6d49b1_2.

5. "Declaring a National Emergency Concerning the Novel Coronavirus Disease (COVID-19) Outbreak: Proclamation 9994 by the President of the United States of America, March 13, 2020," Homeland Security Digital Library, accessed April 9, 2021, hsdl.org/?collection&id=2481.

6. See Jessie Yeung et al., "March 13 Coronavirus News," CNN, March 13, 2020, edition.cnn.com/world/live-news/coronavirus-outbreak-03-13-20 -intl-hnk/h_9246c96c9eaa48dcfe42b12e7670029a; and "Contagion Live News Network: Coronavirus Updates for March 12, 2020," Contagion Live Infectious Diseases Today, contagionlive.com/news /contagion-live-news-network-coronavirus-updates-for-march-12-2020.

7. Maria Nicola et al., "The Soci-economic Implications of the Coronavirus Pandemic (COVID-19): A Review," *International Journal of Surgery* 78 (2020): 185–93.

8. Rivi Frei-Landau, "'When the Going Get Tough, the Tough Get—Creative': Israeli Jewish Religious Leaders Find Religiously Innovative Ways to Preserve Community Members' Sense of Belonging and Resilience During the COVID-19 Pandemic," *Psychological Trauma: Theory, Research, Practice, and Policy* 12, no. S1 (August 2020): S258–60, psycnet.apa.org/fulltext/2020-41724-001.html.

9. Abdullah A. Algaissi et al., "Preparedness and Response to COVID-19 in Saudi Arabia: Building on MERS Experience," *Journal of Infection and Public Health* 13, no. 6 (June 2020): 834–38, sciencedirect.com/science /article/pii/S1876034120304664?via%3Dihub.

10. Lukasz Sulkowski and Grzegorz Ignatowski, "Impact of COVID-19 Pandemic on Organization of Religious Behaviour in Different Christian Denominations in Poland," Multidisciplinary Digital Publishing Institute, May 19, 2020, mdpi.com/2077-1444/11/5/254/htm.

11. Alexander Paul Isiko, "Religious Construction of Disease: An Exploratory Appraisal of Religious Responses to the COVID-19 Pandemic in Uganda," *Journal of African Studies and Development* 12, no. 3 (July–September 2020): 77–96.

12. "In One Month, STOP AAPI HATE Receives Almost 1500 Incident Reports of Verbal Harassment, Shunning and Physical Assaults," *A3PCON*, April 24, 2020, asianpacificpolicyandplanningcouncil .org/wp-content/uploads/Press_Release_4_23_20.pdf.

13. Erin Donaghue, "2,120 Hate Incidents Against Asian Americans Reported During Coronavirus Pandemic," CBS News, July 2, 2020, cbsnews.com/news/anti-asian-american-hate-incidents-up-racism/.

14. "Donald Trump Calls COVID-19 'Kung Flu' at Rally," Al Jazeera, June 29, 2020, aljazeera.com/programmes/newsfeed/2020/06 /donald-trump-calls-covid-19-kung-flu-rally-200629091258959.html.

15. "Statement on Anti-Asian Racism in the Time of COVID-19," Asian American Christian Collaborative, accessed March 5, 2021, asianamericanchristiancollaborative.com/read-statement.

16. "By, For, and About Asian American Christians," Asian American Christian Collaborative, accessed March 5, 2021, asianamericanchristiancollaborative.com/our-vision.

17. Cecilia Reyes, Nausheen Husain, Christy Gutowski, Stacy St. Clair, and Gregory Pratt, "Chicago's Coronavirus Disparity: Black Chicagoans Are Dying at Nearly Six Times the Rate of White Residents, Data Show,"

Chicago Tribune, April 7, 2020, chicagotribune.com/coronavirus
/ct-coronavirus-chicago-coronavirus-deaths-demographics-lightfoot
-20200406-77nlylhiavgjzb2wa4ckivh7mu-story.html.

18. Ravina Kullar et al., "Racial Disparity of Coronavirus Disease 2019 in African American Communities," *The Journal of Infectious Diseases* 222, no. 6 (August 2020): 890–93.

19. Ala L. Alkhatib et al., "BMI Is Associated with Coronavirus Disease 2019 Intensive Care Unit Admission in African Americans," *Obesity* 28, no. 10 (October 2020): 1798–1801, onlinelibrary.wiley.com/doi/pdf /10.1002/oby.22937.

20. Christina Carrega and Lakeia Brown, "Sorrowful: Black Clergy Members and Churches Reeling from COVID-19 Losses," ABC News, May 21, 2020, abcnews.go.com/US/sorrowful-black-clergy-members-churches -reeling-covid-19/story?id=70434181.

21. Elaine Howard Ecklund and Deidra Carroll Coleman, "It's Hard to Close Black Churches amid COVID-19: African American Clergy Respond to Pandemic with Unique Considerations of Culture, History, and Faith Values," *Christianity Today*, March 24, 2020, christianitytoday.com/ct/2020/march-web-only/coronavirus-hard -to-close-black-churches-amid-covid-19.html.

22. Lauren Victoria Burke, "COVID-19: Black Churches Employ Innovation to Worship During a Pandemic," *Jacksonville Free Press*, April 1, 2020, jacksonvillefreepress.com/covid-19-black-churches-employ-innovation -to-worship-during-a-pandemic/.

23. Carlos E. Rodriguez-Dias et al., "Risk for COVID-19 Infection and Death among Latinos in the United States: Examining Heterogeneity in Transmission Dynamics," *Annals of Epidemiology* 52 (December 2020): 46–53.e2.

24. Celine McNicholas and Margaret Poydock, "Who Are Essential Workers?: A Comprehensive Look at Their Wages, Demographics, and Unionization Rates," Economic Policy Institute, May 19, 2020, epi.org/blog/who-are -essential-workers-a-comprehensive-look-at-their-wages-demographics -and-unionization-rates/.

25. Rodriguez-Dias et al., "Risk for COVID-19 Infection."

26. Celia Falicov, Alba Niño, and Maria Sol D'Urso, "Expanding Possibilities: Flexibilities and Solidarity with Under Resourced Immigrant Families During the COVID-19 Pandemic," *Family Process* 59, no. 3 (September 2020): 872, onlinelibrary.wiley.com/doi/10.1111/famp.12578.

27. Rodolfo Galvan Estrada III, "'Free in Christ' to Defy State Closures? Latino Churches Offer Insight," *Christianity Today*, May 22, 2020,

christianitytoday.com/ct/2020/may-web-only/covid-free-in-christ-to
-defy-state-closures-latino-churches.html.

28. David Roach, "Christian Giving Rebounds to Pre-Pandemic Levels,"
    Christianity Today, June 11, 2020, christianitytoday.com/news/2020
    /june/ecfa-coronavirus-church-ministry-giving-finances.html.

29. See "Churches and Faith-Based Organizations May Apply for CARES Act
    Loans," Church and Tax Law Update, April 4, 2020, churchlawandtax
    .com/web/2020/april/churches-and-faith-based-organizations-may
    -apply-for-cares-.html; and Bob Turner, "Footnotes: Church, Money, and
    COVID-19," Harding University, March 20, 2020, scholarworks.harding
    .edu/cgi/viewcontent.cgi?article=1037&context=hst-footnotes.

30. "Resources for Coronavirus COVID-19 Economic Impact," Crown,
    accessed March 9, 2021, crown.org/coronavirus/.

31. "Cru Inner City COVID-19 Response," Cru.org, accessed March 9,
    2021, cru.org/us/en/communities/innercity/media/covid-19
    -response.html.

32. "YFC Houston Celebrates Workers in the Juvenile System," Youth for
    Christ, September 23, 2020, yfc.net/stories/yfc-houston-celebrates
    -workers-in-the-juvenile-justice-system.

33. Some of the featured stories are: Tess Schoonhoven, "3-Member Church
    Closed During COVID-19 Finds New Life," NAMB, May 21, 2020,
    namb.net/news/3-member-church-closed-during-covid-19-finds-new
    -life/; Tobin Perry, "Some Camps Going Digital to Reach and Mobilize
    Students This Summer," NAMB, May 29, 2020, namb.net/news/some
    -camps-going-digitial-to-reach-and-mobilize-students-this-summer/;
    and Brandon Elrod, "Southern Baptist Military Chaplains Minister in
    the Face of COVID-19," NAMB, March 13, 2020, namb.net/news
    /southern-baptist-military-chaplains-minister-in-the-face-of-covid-19/.

34. Nigel Yates, *Liturgical Space: Christian Worship and Church Buildings in
    Western Europe 1500–2000* (Burlington, VT: Ashgate, 2008), 2–3.

35. "COVID-19: How Can Churches Respond?," Anglican Alliance,
    accessed March 9, 2021, anglicanalliance.org/covid-19-how-can
    -churches-respond/.

36. Jamie Aten and Kent Annan, "Preparing Your Church for Coronavirus
    (COVID-19): A Step-by-Step, Research-Informed and Faith-Based
    Planning Manual," Humanitarian Disaster Institute, accessed March 9,
    2021, wheaton.edu/media/humanitarian-disaster-institute/Preparing
    -Your-Church-for-Coronavirus.pdf.

37. Episcopal Relief & Development, "The Rev. Glenna Huber, Rev.
    Kim Jackson and Aaron Scott Discuss How COVID-19 Has Affected

Homeless Communities," COVID-19 Webinar Series, May 15, 2020, episcopalrelief.org/what-we-do/us-disaster-program/faith-based -response-to-epidemics/on-the-topic-of-epidemics/covidand homelesscommunities/.

38. For more information on these prayer gatherings see, facebook.com /LongBeachChurchCollective.

39. D. A. Horton, "Holistic and Locally Present Engagement: A Near-Term Analysis," Send Institute, June 23, 2020, sendinstitute.org/holistic -locally-present-engagement-short-term-analysis/.

CHAPTER 3: CRISIS WHILE THE WORLD MARCHES ON

1. Michael O. Emerson and Christian Smith, *Divided by Faith: Evangelical Religion and the Problem of Race in America* (Oxford: University Press, 2000), 21–22.

2. Joseph Evans, *Reconciliation and Reparation: Preaching Economic Justice* (Valley Forge, PA: Judson Press, 2018), 5.

3. Evans, *Reconciliation and Reparation*, 5.

4. Black Lives Matter (BLM) is both a social movement and the name of a global organization. Not everyone who supports the social movement is affiliated with the global organization or its methods.

5. J. Deotis Roberts, *A Black Political Theology* (Louisville, KY: Westminster John Knox Press, 2005), 220.

6. Roberts, *Black Political Theology*, 221.

7. Roberts, *Black Political Theology*, 85.

8. Samuel George Hines and Curtiss Paul DeYoung with Dalineta L. Hines, *Beyond Rhetoric: Reconciliation as a Way of Life* (Eugene, OR: Wipf and Stock, 2011), xxii.

CHAPTER 4: A BRIEF HISTORY OF CRISIS

1. Bruce L. Shelley and Marshall Shelley, *Church History in Plain Language*, 5th ed. (Nashville: Thomas Nelson, 2020), 3. Much of the straight history presented in this chapter is adapted from my work on the fifth edition of this classic text.

2. As quoted in Shelley, *Church History*, 133.

3. As quoted in Shelley, *Church History*, 140.

4. Charles L. Mee Jr., *The Black Death* (Boston: New Word City, 2014).

5. Samuel Cohn and Tom Beaumont James, "Black Death Facts: Your Guide to 'the Worst Catastrophe in Recorded History,'" HistoryExtra, May 12, 2020, historyextra.com/period/medieval/black-death-plague -epidemic-facts-what-caused-rats-fleas-how-many-died/.

6. Barbara W. Tuchman, *A Distant Mirror: The Calamitous 14th Century* (New York: Ballantine Books, 1979), 96.

7. Tuchman, *Distant Mirror*, 97.

8. John Kelly, *The Great Mortality: An Intimate History of the Black Death, the Most Devastating Plague of All Time* (New York: HarperCollins, 2005), 222.

9. Tuchman, *Distant Mirror*, 97.

10. Philip Ziegler, *The Black Death* (New York: HarperPerennial, 2009), 262.

11. Raymond Henry Payne Crawfurd, *Plague and Pestilence in Literature and Art* (Oxford: Clarendon Press, 1914), 122.

12. Mark Galli, "When a Third of the World Died," Christian History Institute, accessed April 8, 2021, christianhistoryinstitute.org/magazine /article/when-a-third-of-the-world-died.

13. Tuchman, *Distant Mirror*, 123.

14. Julian of Norwich, *Revelations of Divine Love* (New York: Penguin Books, 1998), 22.

15. Julian of Norwich, *Revelations*, 38.

16. Tim Serban, "Prayer Service for the 10th Anniversary of 9/11" *Vision* 21, no. 5 (September/October 2011): 22, nacc.org/wp-content /uploads/2015/12/NACC_Vision_Sept-Oct_2011.pdf.

17. John Starke, "New York's Post-9/11 Church Boom," The Gospel Coalition, September 7, 2011, thegospelcoalition.org/article /new-yorks-post-911-church-boom/.

18. Starke, "Post-9/11 Church Boom."

19. Tony Carnes, "Part 8: The Making of the Postsecular City: The West Side Story," NYRC Religion, December 20, 2010, nycreligion.info /part-8-making-postsecular-city-west-side-story/.

20. Starke, "Post-9/11 Church Boom."

21. Eric Ferreri, "After 9/11, a Short-lived Rush to Church," *Duke Today*, August 19, 2016, today.duke.edu/2016/08/after-911-short-lived -rush-church.

22. Vernon Grounds, personal correspondence to Denver Seminary supporters, December 2001.

23. Grounds, personal correspondence.

24. *Select Lectures Comprising Some of the More Valuable Lectures Delivered before the Young Men's Christian Association in Exeter Hall, London, from 1847 to 1855*, ed. D. W. Clark (Cincinnati: L. Swormstedt & A. Poe, 1856), 71.

25. Billy Graham, "On Technology and Faith," filmed February 1998 in

Monterey, CA, TED video, 26:07, ted.com/talks/billy_graham_on
_technology_and_faith#t-19918.

CHAPTER 5: THE BIBLE'S CATALOG OF CRISIS

1. Jeremiah's other contribution to the canon of Scripture is the book of
   Lamentations, another tear-stained document. Soong-Chan Rah has
   written an excellent commentary on that book, which I commend to
   you: *Prophetic Lament: A Call for Justice in Troubled Times* (Downers
   Grove, IL: IVP Books, 2015).
2. Seth Godin, "When Can We Talk About Our Systems?," blog,
   September 24, 2020, seths.blog/2020/09/when-can-we-talk
   -about-your-system/.
3. "Protests and the Pandemic with Michele Norris," *The Michelle
   Obama Podcast,* August 2020, open.spotify.com/episode
   /0ASSMnYfKKdTpsyUUPHbli.

CHAPTER 6: JESUS WOULDN'T WASTE A CRISIS

1. *A Year with C. S. Lewis: Daily Readings from His Classic Works,* ed.
   Patricia S. Klein (San Francisco: HarperSanFrancisco, 2003), 309.
2. Jill Jonnes, *Eiffel's Tower: And the World's Fair Where Buffalo Bill
   Beguiled Paris, the Artists Quarreled, and Thomas Edison Became
   a Count* (New York: Viking, 2009), 199.
3. Glenn Packiam, "Science and Scripture Agree: Singing Lifts Our
   Spirits," *Christianity Today,* June 22, 2020, christianitytoday.com
   /ct/2020/july-august/glenn-packiam-worship-world-come-singing
   -hope.html.
4. Ada R. Habershon, "He Will Hold Me Fast," 1908. Public domain.

CHAPTER 7: A SPIRITUALITY OF CRISIS RESPONSE

1. All citations in this chapter, unless otherwise indicated, are from Glenn
   Packiam, "Five Things to Know About Lament," N. T. Wright Online,
   accessed March 16, 2021, https://www.ntwrightonline.org/five-things
   -to-know-about-lament.

CHAPTER 8: GROWING A CHURCH IN THE RUINS

1. Derek Thompson, "How Disaster Shaped the Modern City," *The
   Atlantic,* October 2020. This article is accessible online with the title
   "Get Ready for the Great Urban Comeback," theatlantic.com/magazine
   /archive/2020/10/how-disaster-shaped-the-modern-city/615484/.
2. Thompson, "How Disaster Shaped the Modern City."

3. Michael Frost and Alan Hirsch, *The Shaping of Things to Come: Innovation and Mission for the 21st-Century Church*, rev. and updated ed. (Grand Rapids, MI: Baker Books, 2013).

4. As noted in David Kinnaman and Aly Hawkins, *You Lost Me: Why Young Christians Are Leaving Church . . . and Rethinking Faith* (Grand Rapids, MI: Baker Books, 2016).

5. Thom Schultz, "The Rise of the Dones: The 'Done With Church' Population," ChurchLeaders, January 28, 2020, churchleaders.com /outreach-missions/outreach-missions-articles/177144-thom-schultz -rise-of-the-done-with-church-population.html.

6. Schultz, "Rise of the Dones."

7. Nate Pyle (@NatePyle79), Twitter post, September 7, 2020, twitter.com/NatePyle79/status/1303163352923942915.

8. See Jemar Tisby, *The Color of Compromise: The Truth about the American Church's Complicity in Racism* (Grand Rapids, MI: Zondervan, 2019).

9. Kinnaman and Hawkins, *You Lost Me*, 54–55.

10. David J. Bosch, *Transforming Mission: Paradigm Shifts in Theology of Mission*, 20th anniversary ed., American Society of Missiology Series, no. 16 (Maryknoll, NY: Orbis Books, 2011), 2.

11. Bosch, *Transforming Mission*, 2–3.

12. See Roland Allen, *The Spontaneous Expansion of the Church: And the Causes Which Hinder It* (Grand Rapids, MI: Eerdmans, 1962).

13. See JR Woodward and Dan White Jr., *The Church as Movement: Starting and Sustaining Missional-Incarnational Communities* (Downers Grove, IL: IVP Books, 2016).

14. Alan Hirsch, *The Forgotten Ways: Reactivating Apostolic Movements*, 2nd ed. (Grand Rapids, MI: Brazos Press, 2016).

15. Hirsch, *Forgotten Ways*, 48.

16. See Tod Bolsinger, *Leadership for a Time of Pandemic: Practicing Resilience* (Downers Grove, IL: InterVarsity Press, 2020), 5.

17. David Brooks, "The Nuclear Family Was a Mistake," *The Atlantic*, March 2020, theatlantic.com/magazine/archive/2020/03/the-nuclear -family-was-a-mistake/605536/.

18. It is interesting to note here that the more formalized Communion arose as churches became more institutionalized and depersonalized; the early church, which had yet to grow numerically and was based in households, conducted its Communions in a form that is now identified as love feasts. See Alan Kreider, *The Patient Ferment of the Early Church: The Improbable Rise of Christianity in the Roman Empire* (Grand Rapids, MI: Baker Academic, 2016).

19. Another way to conceptualize this difference is to examine spaces of belonging. To focus on Sunday worship broadcasts is to choose the *public space* (a group of seventy plus) as the main sphere of ministry, but to focus on building community means to emphasize a smaller gathering, often the *personal space* (a group of five to twelve). Focus on public space is a feature of Christendom mode, whereas focus on the personal space is a feature of missional ministry in the post-Christendom era. See Woodward and White, *Church as Movement*, 155–60.

20. Robert Lupton, "Good Christians—Lousy Neighbors!" FCS Urban Ministries, June 1994, fcsministries.org/urban-perspectives/good -christians-lousy-neighbors/. Note: Page no longer exists.

21. See Tom Gjelten, "Multiracial Congregations May Not Bridge Racial Divide," NPR, July 17, 2020, npr.org/2020/07/17/891600067 /multiracial-congregations-may-not-bridge-racial-divide/.

CHAPTER 9: HE HAS SHOWN US WHAT IS GOOD

1. Learn more about how to practice the Prayer of Examen on pages 42–43 in Catherine McNiel, *All Shall Be Well: Awakening to God's Presence in His Messy, Abundant World* (Colorado Springs: NavPress, 2019).

2. An excellent resource for lament is Aubrey Sampson, *The Louder Song: Listening for Hope in the Midst of Lament* (Colorado Springs: NavPress, 2019).

CHAPTER 10: GOD REMAINS GOOD

1. The story of Mary, Martha, and their brother is found in John 11.

2. Michael Card, "Job Suite," *The Way of Wisdom* © 1990 Sparrow Records.

CONTRIBUTORS

LEE ECLOV served as a pastor for forty years. He is an adjunct professor at Trinity Evangelical Divinity School and has been a regular contributor to PreachingToday.com, *Leadership Journal*, and CTPastors.com. His books include *Pastoral Graces: Reflections on the Care of Souls* and *Feels Like Home: How Rediscovering the Church as Family Changes Everything* (both Moody).

SEAN GLADDING is the author of *The Story of God, the Story of Us* and *TEN* (both IVP) and *A View from the Margins: Stories for Holy Week*. His family lives in Lexington, Kentucky.

D. A. HORTON is an assistant professor and director of the Intercultural Studies program at California Baptist University. He serves as an associate teaching pastor at The Grove Community Church in Riverside, California. He and his wife, Elicia, have been married for seventeen years and have three kids.

CHRISTINE JESKE researches and writes about the ways people seek the good life in settings ranging from South African workplaces to Wisconsin small farms. She teaches cultural anthropology at Wheaton College and is the author of several books, including *Into the Mud* (Moody) and *The Laziness Myth* (Cornell University Press).

KYUBOEM LEE was raised in South Korea and Kenya and has lived in Philadelphia since 1993, where he has ministered and church planted cross-culturally. He teaches at Missio Seminary, coaches church planters with V3, and edits the *Journal of Urban Mission*.

JO ANNE LYON is an ordained minister in The Wesleyan Church, serving eight years as global general superintendent. She is the founder of World Hope International, a relief and development agency, and serves as vice chair of the Board of the National Association of Evangelicals.

CATHERINE MCNIEL is the author of *All Shall Be Well: Awakening to God's Presence in His Messy, Abundant World* and *Long Days of Small Things: Motherhood as a Spiritual Discipline* (both NavPress).

MATT MIKALATOS is a minister, speaker, and author. His most recent nonfiction book is *Journey to Love: What We Long For, How to Find It, and How to Pass It On*. He's also the author of the fantasy novel *The Crescent Stone*. Learn more at www.mikalatos.com.

MARSHALL SHELLEY is former VP of *Christianity Today* and is author of *Ministering to Problem People in Your Church* (Bethany House), general editor of *The Quest Study Bible* (Zondervan), coauthor of *The Leadership Secrets of Billy Graham* (Zondervan), and coauthor with his father, church historian Bruce Shelley, of *Church History in Plain Language*, 5th ed. (Zondervan).

EFREM SMITH is co-senior pastor of Bayside Church Midtown in Sacramento, CA, and co-owner of Influential LLC, a speaking, coaching, and consulting company. He is the author of *The Post-Black and Post-White Church* (Jossey-Bass) as well as *Killing Us Softly* (NavPress).

ANGIE WARD is a teacher and author with nearly thirty years of experience in church, parachurch, and higher-education ministry. She is the author of *I Am a Leader: When Women Discover the Joy of their Calling* (NavPress) and serves as assistant director of the Doctor of Ministry program at Denver Seminary.

ABOUT KINGDOM CONVERSATIONS

TO BE A CHRISTIAN is to be conscious of and responsive to three realities at once: the past, the present, and the future.

We pay attention to the *past*, understanding that God has spoken to those who have gone before us, giving practical instruction for a way of being in the world. We learn what it means to be a peculiar people with the privilege of calling God our Father.

We pay attention to the *future*, recognizing that God has invited us to participate in his coming resolution to all the world's pain and suffering.

And we pay attention to the *present* because the present is where we live, move, and have our being.

Still, we are often distracted by crises and conundrums, and we forget to look to the past to inform us, to the future to inspire us, even to the facts on the ground present to us. But when we step back to consider the vantage point of our good God, who is the same yesterday, today, and forever, these circumstances take their proper shape and size in our imaginations, and we find our footing and our way of glorifying God in our response.

Kingdom Conversations are meant to facilitate this exercise in finding our footing. We dare to consider that any issue, no matter how complex, may be brought into conversation with what we know of God and of history and of one another, and in so doing, we can find new insight into how the people of God can persevere and bless through the great complexities of our time.

They are "conversations" because they gather the perspectives of various Christian leaders to consider the question together.

They are "Kingdom" because they are each submitted in humility and hope to God, trusting that God himself will lead us into all truth.